D0065724

FIDDLERS AND WHORES

James Lowry's surgical instruments in their original case.

Fiddlers and Whores

The Candid Memoirs of a Surgeon in Nelson's Fleet

by JAMES LOWRY

Edited and Introduced by John Millyard

"It is a country of fiddlers and poets, whores and
scoundrels"
– Nelson on Naples, 1798

CHATHAM PUBLISHING

LONDON

Introduction copyright © John Millyard 2006

First published in Great Britain in 2006 by
Chatham Publishing
Lionel Leventhal Ltd,
Park House, 1 Russell Gardens,
London NW11 9NN

British Library Cataloguing in Publication Data
Lowry, James
Fiddlers and whores : the candid memoirs of a surgeon in
Nelson's fleet
1. Lowry, James 2. Great Britain. Royal Navy – History –
18th century 3. Great Britain. Royal Navy – Military life
4. Great Britain. Royal Navy – Surgeons 5. Second
Coalition, War of the, 1798–1801 – Personal narratives,
British 6. Ship physicians – Great Britain – Anecdotes
I. Title
940.2′745′092

ISBN-13: 9781861762689
ISBN-10: 1861762682
ISBN 1 86176 268 2

Designed and Typeset by Servis Filmsetting Ltd, Manchester
Printed and bound by Cromwell Press Ltd, Wilts

Contents

This book is dedicated to the late Jean Dorothy Stewart, great, great, great grandniece of Dr James Lowry. As the family historian, it was her greatest wish to have his diary published.

Publisher's Note

WHAT FOLLOWS IS SUBSTANTIALLY as Lowry wrote it, with nothing deleted and only the very occasional conjunction or preposition added where the sense obviously requires it. However, his sentences frequently ramble and are often ungrammatical, so modern punctuation has been added or the original altered where necessary to clarify the author's meaning.

Lowry's inconsistent spelling of common words has been modernised, but his own versions of place names and people have been retained, as has most of his idiosyncratic vocabulary. For example, he sometimes uses 'rout' in its modern sense but at other times to mean 'route'. His exuberant and anarchic employment of capitals has also been toned down.

The principal impositions of this edition are the chapter structure and the title – clearly inappropriate to the extended personal letter written by Lowry, but essential way-marks in a printed book.

Introduction

GETTING JAMES LOWRY'S JOURNAL into print has for
me been a labour of love with an exceedingly long
gestation time. I first conceived the possibility more
than a dozen years ago, around 1990, when research-
ing and writing a corporate history of a family-owned
publishing company in Toronto. In the process, I
interviewed Dorothy Stewart, an elderly woman who
was related to the company's founder.

Crippled in her youth by the scourge of polio that
ran rampant in Canada during the first half of the
twentieth century, Dorothy was nevertheless charming and cooperative. During our chat she mentioned
offhand that she had squirrelled away something
interesting written by another relative, her great,
great grandfather's brother. She rolled her wheel-
chair across the room and from a cupboard dug out
an old journal. It was about 250 closely handwritten
pages, browning with age between two pieces of stiff
cardboard and held together with frayed string. She
followed that up with a wooden box almost two feet
long and fitted with two-tiered velvet inlays encasing
a set of extremely old medical instruments.

It was truly exciting to touch these old pages and read the words that a young Irish physician had penned for his brother at the peak of Britain's struggle against Napoleon, and which highlighted one of Napoleon's primary nemeses, Admiral Lord Nelson. Those words vividly and idiosyncratically described a world that existed almost 200 years before – not a fabricated world created by a novelist's imagination, but a very real, very authentic and tangible one as seen though the eyes of James Lowry, a young man who had actually lived the words and deeds he documented in these yellowing pages.

The classically educated young man-turned-ship's-surgeon in Lord Nelson's Mediterranean fleet jotted down observations both of his adventures afloat and his military and romantic conquests ashore. He was intrigued by the varied peoples and customs he observed in all the countries and ports of call he visited during his six years in a Royal Navy that much of the time was battling the French under Napoleon.

Unfortunately, Dr Lowry's ship was savaged by a ferocious storm as he returned to England after six years away, and he lost his original diary and sketches in the wreck. Fortunately rescued, he retired from the navy after he reached home and settled down in the seaside town of Deal in Kent, practising medicine. He then reconstructed this account from memory to send to his clergyman brother in Ireland, to pass on some idea of the exciting (and sometimes bloody) experiences of his time at sea, not to mention the romantic liaisons on land. He later moved to Maidstone, where he died in 1855.

Lowry never mentions in the journal what prompted him to leave home and hearth as an eighteen-year-old to take part in the momentous struggle that was threatening Britain (which at that time included Ireland). Napoleon was on the rampage in Europe, so perhaps being young and patriotic, Lowry was eager to participate in the fight against the French. Though fresh from schooling in the classics, he may well have conceived the idea that a quick medical course would provide an agreeable shortcut to becoming qualified for admission to the Royal Navy as an officer.

The service Lowry joined was reaching the pinnacle of its efficiency and success, and he was to become personally involved in some of the most significant events of a long naval war. By the time he went to sea, the armies of the revolutionary French republic were everywhere successful on the European mainland. As a result, Britain lived with the constant threat of invasion, if not by direct assault across the Channel, then through the 'back door' opened by civil unrest in Ireland. Indeed, Lowry's first taste of action was against a French expedition attempting to land troops and arms to support an Irish insurrection. The complete destruction and dispersal of this force in October 1798 was an indicator of the growing disparity between the effectiveness of the Royal Navy and its French counterpart.

Like many a landsman before him, Lowry registers astonishment, and initial distaste, at living conditions aboard his first ship; but to be fair, this is an accommodation hulk, and once he joins a commissioned warship we hear little of the discomfort, poor victuals and draconian discipline that was supposedly the lot of the Georgian sailor. Admittedly, as even a junior officer, he was entitled to privileges which included private catering, and he noted the difference when occasionally circumstances reduced him to 'the King's allowance'. However, he never mentions diet-related disorders among his patients, who at every stage of his career seem to be mostly what he terms 'venereals'. By Lowry's time that great scourge of ocean voyaging, scurvy, had been virtually conquered in the Royal Navy; caused by Vitamin C deficiency, it was kept at bay by a regulation issue of lime juice.

Another surprising omission is the lack of reference to punishment. Part of the surgeon's regular duties was to attend floggings, to ensure that the subject was fit to take his sentence. Many later accounts of naval life of the period note with horror the effect of witnessing the first flogging, but not Lowry's. He may have been exceptionally fortunate in the captains he served under, but he must have seen the cat-o'nine-tails in action on at least a few occasions. Even though he was a professional medical man, he was not insensitive to suffering – he was much moved by the plight of the wounded after battles in Egypt, for example – so one can only conclude that flogging was not as shocking to the contemporary sensibility as so many Victorian published memoirs would have us think.

The one aspect unique to naval service that Lowry refers to again and again is the system of prize money. Captured ships and their cargoes were sold and the proceeds divided among the crews of the victorious ships. Nowadays we might see this as an incentive scheme, but one that might tempt an officer to put profit above duty. This was a matter of debate even at the time, and it is clear from Lowry's testimony that even modest success could alter an officer's finances dramatically, perhaps producing a year's salary from a single capture. In fact, Lowry encountered one of fortune's greatest favourites in the captain of the frigate *Medusa*, John Gore. He was involved in two of the greatest-ever hauls of Spanish treasure, in 1799 and 1804, and later took a hugely valuable cargo of quicksilver, netting in total something like 600 times his annual salary and making him in modern terms a multi-millionaire. He could well afford the lavish ball he held aboard his ship to entertain the Neapolitan court.

Judged on its historical significance, Lowry's account of his time in the Mediterranean fleet is probably the most interesting part of his memoirs – as much for what he does not choose to say, as the subjects that do take his interest. This was the period just after Nelson's great victory at the Nile, when he was being feted by all of Neapolitan society from the king and queen downwards. According to some accounts of his life, the flattery turned his head and ruined his judgement, eventually leading to what many historians regard as the greatest stain on Nelson's reputation: his involvement in the execution of Prince Caracciolo, a Neapolitan naval officer who had served the rebel Jacobin regime. If Lowry felt there was anything untoward or reprehensible in Nelson's conduct, he does not mention it; but he does have one grisly story that underlines the viciousness of the Neapolitan civil war into which British naval forces had been drawn. He also confirms the unlikely-sounding story of the corpse of Caracciolo surfacing alongside the *Foudroyant* under the nose of a startled King Ferdinand, who happened to be aboard. There are other versions of this tale, but only Lowry explains how it was achieved.

Famously, this is also the time when Nelson began

his affair with Lady Hamilton, yet, writing in 1807, Lowry did not assume that his brother knew who she was. Possibly gossip was slow to reach rural Ireland, but Lowry would have had to make mention of the relationship if it were common knowledge. It is not that he was is in any way coy: indeed, the tales of his own amorous adventures verge on boasting. Like many British officers from a relatively buttoned-up society, he found the sexual mores of Italy as startling as they were seductive. Not surprisingly, much of Lowry's narrative is devoted to his exploration of this mind-broadening experience.

Lowry was lucky to have the short-lived period of the Peace of Amiens to follow his shoreside pursuits, which included many of the fashionable artistic and intellectual interests of the period. In fact his extensive visits to the antiquities of Pompeii, Sicily and the Holy Land virtually formed a poor man's Grand Tour. His observations reveal an enquiring and sceptical frame of mind, but he was not enthralled by the wonders of the orient as were so many of his contemporaries like Byron or Lady Hester Stanhope.

His service afloat was also varied, but perhaps not untypical of a naval career in those years. Besides the obvious workings of seapower, the navy was much employed in amphibious warfare, something Lowry saw at close quarters. He was present at the abortive attack on Cadiz in 1800, but the following year joined the army ashore in the far more successful campaign in Egypt which eventually saw the defeat of Napoleon's veterans, although Bonaparte himself had long since escaped to France.

Lowry was not present at the French surrender either, having been ordered home in a worn-out 74-gun ship, the *Swiftsure*. This ship suffered the unusual fate for a British battleship of being captured, and for a brief period Lowry was a prisoner of war. French prize crews had a reputation for ill-discipline and looting, and Lowry's clothes-trunk was stolen even as he was tending the wounded. Although the culprits were apprehended rapidly, their attempts to take revenge nearly proved fatal to all in the ship. Once in Toulon, however, Lowry was well-treated, benefiting from the informal free-masonry of the medical profession. He was also fortunate to be quickly released, since the civilised convention of exchange, whereby prisoners were repatriated in return for someone of equivalent rank, was still observed by the French republic. Napoleon later abrogated this agreement, condemning thousands of captives to long-term incarceration in the insanitary prison-hulks of Britain or the dank fortresses of France.

Lowry's last great adventure was the wreck of the brig *Weazle* in March 1804. In general, British seamen of this era were statistically more likely to suffer from what the Naval Prayer calls the 'dangers of the sea' than the 'violence of the enemy', but it was no less traumatic for being commonplace. Having miraculously escaped with his life, at this point Lowry decided to give up the sea, and after an eventful journey reached Ireland in June 1804. His six-year service had been full of variety and incident, summarised by Lowry himself on setting foot on his native soil:

> I entered into a soliloquy, thanking the Father of Mercies for my safe arrival, and congratulating myself on having the opportunity and the pleasure of seeing a great part of the three quarters of the Globe, Europe, Africa and Asia, beside a great number of islands – Minorca, Majorca, St. Peters, Malta, Lampadosa, Sicily, Corsica, Elba, Candia, Cyprus, Rhodes – and several other places, both on the Continent and lesser islands, but as nothing particular occurred to me, I did not conceive it worthy of inserting. I likewise had the honour to be in several desperate battles, both by sea and land, against the enemies of my country, the misfortune to be taken prisoner into France and was very near being blown up by powder, likewise shipwrecked and the fortune to have escaped multitudes of dangers which of course was incident to my way of life, in travelling the sea several hundred thousands

of miles which would puzzle a better mathematician than me to calculate; and the two last, although best, a series of good health in all the various climes, and the luck to increase my fortune.

James Lowry never married and had no children. This record of a youthful period of his life must have been passed on by James's brother, Rev. John Lowry, who at one time was the minister of Lower Clonaneese Presbyterian Church, Castlecaulfield, County Tyrone, Ireland. Somehow it made its way to North America.

At some point before the 1960s, the journal and instruments reached California (family records suggest that somewhere along the line one of John's descendants, possibly named Jarvie, married an American woman).

Subsequently, in the 1960s, they reached the hands of Hamilton James Stuart, a prominent Toronto Q.C., uncle of Dorothy Stewart and great grandson of the Rev. John Lowry, James's brother.

Ham Stuart, now deceased, became aware of the Lowry journal from an elderly aunt of his, the last of her branch of the Lowry family, who had lived in California with her bachelor brother. After his death, while preparing to leave the home they had shared, she became curious about an old discarded book she noticed on top of the inevitable garden bonfire of accumulated disposables. She plucked it off before it burned. Because of her inquisitive nature, James Lowry was again rescued, this time from the flames.

Two dramatic rescues are enough for any man's life. The time has come to rescue him once and for all from shipwrecks, bonfires, linen cupboards and sub-urban Toronto garages (where he last lay fallow) so he can finally share with a broader audience his fascinating thoughts, observations and adventures in a world now long gone.

JOHN MILLYARD
Toronto, November 2005

Author's Preface

Dear Brother:

You having expressed it would be a gratification to receive a short history of my life, during my departure from Ireland until my return, I now embrace the pleasure of transmitting the following pages.

In my first career I took notes of my proceedings, but unfortunately lost them all at the time of my shipwreck, which no doubt will plead an excuse for its deficiency, as the following short account was entirely deducted from my memory and written on board a ship attended with continual noise and dissipation around me, where I had no solitary retirement or lonely path, which you know is necessary for a composition of this kind to stimulate and impress the memory of past events. Under these disadvantageous circumstances, should it be entertaining to you, and my nearest relations it will highly gratify and amply reward me for the little trouble I have had to recapitulate and render both felicity and satisfaction.

I have taken care not to wander from the truth; my anxiety for such induced me to insert all my juvenile frolics and foibles and several other things, which upon a second consideration ought not to have been introduced. Had I not lost my notes and was desirous, I had plenty of matter to have written volumes, but prolixity was contradictory to my wishes. In one sentence when relating my history, in the next I remove several hundreds of miles without any account of my passage for the sake of abbreviation and it is necessary for the reader to pay attention to this and consider the distance betwixt each place. In the following lines I have been obliged to adhere to brevity as nothing could make such an indelible impression upon my memory as the remarkable events which never can be erased. The remaining sheets I shall fill at a future period with a continuation of my life which seems as yet to have been the most critical part, my departure from Ireland, the serious accident and my excursions in Germany, etc.

I am with the sincerest esteem,
  Your Brother, [1]

To the
  Rev. Jn[o.] Lowry
    Claniniss[2]
1st July 1807,
  Deal[3] in Kent, England.

1. Leaving Ireland, 1797

IN THE YEAR 1797[4] after learning the Latin and Greek, I proceeded on my Journey to Belfast where I procured a passage to Greenock; contrary winds prevented us from going farther than Carrickfergus, where we anchored, and the winds always continuing foul, we were obliged to delay five days and then proceeded on our course to Scotland. It blew very fresh, and being a slanting wind, it was three days more before we landed. Our small sea stock (which was only laid in for thirty hours) was all exhausted. The whole of the passengers (seventeen students) were sick; I was the only one that escaped it. Of course I lived and fared sumptuously upon our provisions, until the last day, at which time the sea sickness left them. They had voracious appetites and devoured the remainder in a very short time.

I have remarked since I have belonged to the watery element that those who have been attacked with sea sickness always, on their recovery, had very sharp appetites and in the intervals of their illness would have a great craving for food, but on taking the least quantity would instantly vomit it. The captain was a very ignorant, uncouth being, would not supply our craving appetites. Per force and strength of arms we made him hoist the boat out and land us four miles distant from Greenock; it was then a calm, about twelve o'clock in the day. Not being able to haul the boat close to the shore, we cast lots who should strip and carry the remainder on their backs to *terra firma*. We continued our course to Glasgow. On the approach of night, we endeavoured to procure lodgings, being very much fatigued. Our party was so numerous, all the innkeepers, I suppose, took us to be a banditti of Irish renegades or a wandering tribe of vagrants. They would hardly permit us to enter their houses, alone give us a night's lodging.

After dark we walked four miles farther, but thought it expedient to separate into parties. At last my friend Parker and another young man with myself entered a house with the intention of not leaving that night; we should at all events try the strength of our arms. Through partly persuasion and intrusion we obtained a room with one bed and a proviso of being locked up like thieves. After our night's repose, the next day we got the length of Glasgow.

I lodged there in a house with a lady; from her melancholy appearance my curiosity was excited to enquire into the cause. Upon an accurate investigation, I learned she had just been cured of a venereal complaint. The following day when I was walking in the clinical ward of the Royal Infirmary, I saw a most emaciated and debilitated man, with his nose decayed off, large blotches on his skin, his breath foetid, a cadaverous smell over all his body. I ascertained with astonishment that he was my landlady's husband. When I became more intimate with her, this pretty young creature related the whole circumstance of marriage and how she became infected with the above disease, but not without great emotions and grief. About three months after matrimony, enjoying all the sweets of a nuptial couch and living in the greatest cordiality, her vitiated husband from mere wantonness had connection with a prostitute, after this baneful contact was infected with the venereal disease. Knowing if he would have connection with his wife would communicate the contagion, he declined for a considerable time, applied to quacks and was under their care for three months. In a state of inebriety he gave the venereal disease to his wife; the nuptial bed then became a bed of sorrow. The complaint increased rapidly and ultimately he went into the infirmary where he had been a few days before I saw him, and died in the most excruciating pains and torture although he had the first medical assistance.

She in a very short time became well, when her

beautiful charms returned. She was endowed with all virtue, humanity and sympathy; in short she was an honour to her sex. What a debauched character he must have been, not to be contented with this charming woman, but must satisfy his lustful desires on the women of the town.

The Divine Providence has wisely ordained this infectious disease. It often proves a great check upon the desires of the wise, and even the libertine, if he wishes to have a sound constitution.

All the winter I made intense application to my professional study, yet by the way of relaxing the mind I often made parties, both of pleasure and study, when we discussed upon different subjects. In a party of the former, I was introduced in a house of pleasure, which being the first time, I may well say the sheep was led to the slaughter. Upon four beautiful young damsels entering the room, adorned in a most handsome and wanton manner, I could not imagine who or what they were, and, as Virgil expressed, my hair stood upon end and I became speechless. In a short time, from their increasing familiarity, immodest gesticulations, I discovered they were prostitutes, or the kind of woman I have heard called as such.

While I remained in Glasgow, there were two instances occurred of tradesmen having their skulls fractured in houses of this description. When I was going very early to college one morning, I saw a young man expiring. Upon enquiring, I learned he would not pay after satiating his desires. They gave him a rap over the head with a poker and then pitched him into an entry. Similar accidents will not happen in the most decent houses, if I am allowed to call them as such. I have heard from gentlemen of great respectability and authenticity, there have been several instances of men throwed out of the high windows of these said houses in Edinburgh and immediately expired. I am happy to learn that such accidents never occur now. My reason for mentioning prostitutes here is that I will not pass over my journeyings without giving a further account of this class of women abroad.

On the 17th of April 1798, I departed from Glasgow, very melancholy after taking leave of my landlady, who I had the pleasure of relating her good qualities before, but now from the generous and friendly behaviour the day previous to my departure will be an inducement for me to be continually interested in her welfare and happiness. She viewed my trunk, where she found a deficiency of accoutrements for travelling and made me a present of eight shirts, waistcoats and neck and pocket handkerchiefs in abundance, likewise a gold ring with her portrait set in it. To my great shame, I never wrote to her as I promised.

My friend, Mr. Cammon accompanied me one mile. After bidding adieu, I commenced a soliloquy, and found myself very much depressed whether my future prospects would turn out to my advantage. Four miles distant from Glasgow, I fell in with a fellow traveller, a butcher, a very entertaining man, which partly prevented the disagreeable thoughts that harassed me. We arrived in Edinburgh that night greatly fatigued after walking forty-four miles.

The subsequent day I proceeded to Leith and took my passage to London. Nothing material happened except very blusterous weather, and was obliged to put in at Berwick upon Tweed, a town upon the borders of England and Scotland. The four ladies, passengers, I sincerely think would have expired from vomiting blood had we not anchored that night. Seven days after my departure from Leith, I arrived in London. The buildings, manners and customs were so different from those of Scotland that they excited many comparative imaginations. At all events, you may walk through the streets at twilight without the danger of domestic slops being dashed over you.

In Scotland there are a great number of families living in the same house, in storey above storey (I do not mean the gentle folk), and they very often throw every filth and nastiness out of the windows upon the streets. Should any person at the time be underneath, he would be nicely besmeared. This custom is more practised in Portugal, where I once saw a young lady dressed in white muslin bedaubed from top to toe. I could scarcely contain laughing at such an instantaneous transfiguration.

When walking up at Wapping Street[5] in the great metropolis, I found my cash to be diminished to £1. 10s. I then began to ruminate: should I not procure a situation or meet with a friend; how should I do for a further supply of that necessary article, money? I introduced my letters of recommendation to two surgeons and one physician. The two former paid very little attention to them; the latter a good deal, but there being no vacancy in an apothecary's shop, they proved to be of no utility, which greatly augmented my anxiety and doubt. I began to lament upon my hard fate and considered myself a madman for my imprudent and rash undertaking under such situated circumstances. However, I had proceeded too far to retreat; a determinated perseverance was my only consolation. I succeeded in obtaining five guineas from a friend, which consoled me for the present.

Now being possessed of a sufficient sum to pass for assistant surgeon in the navy, I thought at all events I would make the attempt. If my mind was harassed before, it now increased twofold whether I should have ability to pass my examination. I studied three weeks in London and then passed my usual examination to my infinite satisfaction at Surgeons Hall and the Sick & Hurt Board.[6]

2. Going to Sea, June 1798

I WAS APPOINTED ASSISTANT surgeon to a very fine ship, the *Foudroyant*,[7] then lying at Plymouth, 270 miles from London. After paying the usual fees for my warrant etc. etc., I was again embarrassed, being reduced to the old sum of £1.10s and the *Foudroyant* at such a distance, I was perplexed with the query, how this would defray my expenses – Perseverance and Necessity, which is the mother of invention, became my motto. I went outside of the stage coach to Portsmouth and then proceeded by sea to Plymouth. I began to calculate my immense wealth, which did not require a day, as it only consisted of threepence, from which sum I purchased a Godly pamphlet.

I joined my ship, without one farthing, the 8th of June 1798. I presented my warrant to the commanding officer, who informed me I must go on board the *Bedford*, an old hulk, as all the officers and ship's company were there and would remain for two or three weeks, until the inside painting of the *Foudroyant* would be dry.

I was introduced in form to my messmates, midshipmen and another surgeon's mate. This being altogether a new scene, I was struck with astonishment. As the *Bedford* was an old hulk and not much trouble taken to keep her clean or purify her decks, the smell was not of the most fragrant kind. On walking down the cockpit ladder, the first thing that struck my olfactory nerves was the long-kept and stinking provisions that the purser's steward was serving out to the sailors. I at last got to the midshipmen's berth by the assistance of a young gentleman that held a light for me.

Being informed that this was our place of abode, I was affected with melancholy amusement that I should have to live in such a gloomy place. (In the cockpit of a line of battle ship, where all the young gentlemen mess, they never have any daylight. All our great naval characters, whether princes or lord's sons, are obliged to be there six years before they are promoted to a lieutenancy.) Casting my eyes around again and viewing the dirty screens, cots and hammocks hanging in all directions, beefsteaks brought on to the table in the same pan they were fried in, and only having two knives amongst the whole of us, I could not avoid imagining them to be singular beings. They informed me that they would not purchase any mess utensils until we should join our new ship, the 'Thunderer', which is the translation for *Foudroyant*, and they would make a subscription and have everything appertaining to make our starboard mess comfortable. Now my whole object was, how I should pay my share of the subscription money and purchase a bed and bedding.

In a few days, contrary to my expectations, I was informed I should be allowed 3d. per mile from Glasgow as conduct money, which amounted to £8.8s.0; this sum came apropos, as it cleared all my expenses for two months. Our surgeon had not joined us but our sick was not numerous; those that were ill were mostly venereals. We had on board 400 prostitutes and of course out of such a number many were diseased. In a short time we were all turned over into the *Foudroyant*, got our berths fitted commodiously, and formed into a regular mess.

It was some time before I got into the habit of sleeping comfortable in those swinging machines (cots).[8] The custom is, when a stranger goes on board (or what they call green horns), to lower them down when asleep. This I found very unpleasant. I jumped out of my cot with an intention of catching the offender but being ignorant of the different windings and in the dark, I stumbled against a stanchion (prop) and bruised myself. Had I caught the gentleman, his head would have felt my vengeance. They very often for fun perform these tricks once or twice, which christens you.

Our captain[9] joined us and we set sail – numerous were the spectators viewing this fine new ship – and went off Brest. We had not cruised long there before we carried away our main top mast in a gale of wind. A short period afterwards we were very close to the French shore when it became a sudden calm, and only for the assistance of boats from the Grand Fleet we should have drifted under their batteries, and been either sunk or rendered ourselves prisoners of war.

After three months cruise we returned to Plymouth to procure water and provisions, where we did not remain long until we got orders of a private nature and departed in the middle of the night to cruise off the coast of Ireland in St. George's Channel. We bespoke a brig that informed us a French squadron full of troops was making the best of their way to land them in Ireland.[10] To our great joy that same evening we saw nine sail of vessels from our mast head. It being nearly dark and very blusterous weather and so near the Irish coast, we had our doubts whether we should come up with the enemy that night, or they might arrive in some contiguous harbour.

Our admiral, Sir Jn⁰· Borlace Warren,[11] made the signal to chase and engage the enemy as each ship came up. The quarters were cleared for action, and the sailors kept at their guns all night. Next morning by daylight we had the fortune to being nearly amongst them. In the night the *La Hoche*, the French admiral's ship, carried away her main top mast, which proved to be a fortunate circumstance as all the French squadron sailed very fast and it would have been a query whether we should have come up with them only for this accident.

His Majesty's Ship *Robust* and *La Hoche*[12] had a smart action, for nearly two hours, at which time the French admiral struck his colours. This exhilarated the spirits of our sailors and gave them additional courage to renew the encounter. The *Foudroyant*, half an hour previous to this, commenced a heavy fire upon several frigates; part struck their colours and part ran away. We had not many men killed or wounded. I was busy, employed in the cockpit stopping the haemorrhages and dressing the wounded. The surgeon and all his assistant surgeons are stationed below (which is out of danger of the balls in the time of battle) where they have a platform made with beds laid on for the convenience of the wounded, all their surgical instruments, bandages, etc. etc. in readiness, and where the officers and sailors are brought to be dressed of their wounds.

The following day we put into the bay called Lough Swilly, within seven miles of Londonderry, Ireland. I was extremely happy of being so near my relations as probably I might have an opportunity to see them. However, I was disappointed. My brother officer (the assistant surgeon) being more of a man of the world, embraced the first opportunity of obtaining permission to see his relations, ten miles from Londonderry; both could not be permitted on account of the number of sick on board. After remaining in this bay for two days, our prizes not having arrived, we went out to look for them. Not falling in with them, we supposed they went into another harbour, therefore we returned again to the same place.

The ladies and gentlemen, hearing we had captured a French squadron with troops on board that intended to land and assist the rebels, flocked from Londonderry and the country adjacent to see our ship. She being the largest that ever was in that bay excited their astonishment. All our officers received very polite invitations to Londonderry. The surgeon's mate having returned, gave me an opportunity of accepting the invitations and enjoy myself in different routs to the above town.

When I deliberated maturely, in fact I had ocular demonstration that I was deficient both in money and clothes which partly obstructed my further pleasure, my accoutrements would answer very well as a student, but in my present condition they were rather shabby comparing them with my companions. After venting my sorrow and passing a few melancholy moments, a more commodious and agreeable way occurred to me (necessity is the mother of invention): that is I would associate with the country farmers and their daughters. I communicated my ideas to a young gentleman who was nearly in the same situation as myself; I found this to be a little consolation. I now passed my time more agreeably and free of expenses in company of a few respectable families near the bay. The Irish hospitality far exceeds any other country, I often heard it remarked by several gentlemen of great erudition and who had made tours through the greatest part of the world. At last the signal was hoisted for all officers to repair on board; I left my female acquaintances with some degree of regret.

We set sail and I bid farewell to my native shore and in a short time we arrived at Plymouth. On our passage the captain died. We preserved his body in spirits, to be interred in England.

We had not remained long at Plymouth until we got orders to fit out for foreign service. I was now reduced to 2d., my shirts all dirty; but the most difficult part was how I should pay a subscription of £10 to defray my mess expenses. These additional embarrassments excited another melancholy reverie. Shortly afterwards, upon inquiry, I found I must serve a year before I would receive any pay, and when on a foreign station, no difference what length of time, I would receive none until my arrival in England – I mean in the capacity of the surgeon's mate. This last intelligence added fuel to the flame and caused numerous unpleasant emotions, but I was a little consoled by my usual motto, 'Patience, Perseverance'.

Upon a consultation with a friend, he advised me to sell my prize money,[13] all our prizes having arrived safely. I went on shore the next day and to my great comfort accomplished it, and procured clothes to the amount of £50, and ready money for my present exigence. This cheered my spirits and drove away all melancholy and gloomy thoughts.

The taking of these ships was as fortunate an incident as ever occurred to me in all my future peregrinations. £60 at this present time was a more essential service than £1000 at any other period, since I now began to think that I had partly succeeded in my old motto, 'Patience and Perseverance'.

After equipping myself with all necessaries of life for a foreign station, we agreed to live on shore and have a dinner or two before or we would leave old England, for which purpose we subscribed seven guineas each. We went to all diversions, such as plays, etc. etc. I must confess I rather lead a life of debauchery.

We made several excursions amongst the ladies of pleasure at Plymouth Dock. Each of my messmates had a fair damsel in keeping for the time we remained there. In the sea port towns in general there is a whole or part of a street inhabited by these amorous fairs, who are very convenient and necessary evils. They live in superb style, have elegant lodgings decorated in the greatest nicety, and their manners rendered extremely pleasing and fascinating by art to attract the eyes of their customers and admirers and likewise to renew and obtain others. Most of the single, and sometimes the married officers, on their arrival from a cruise, not having the society of females for a considerable time, their first object is to pay their respects to these fair but unfortunate damsels.

I cannot pass over without mentioning the transactions of one night but with regret. We all went to the play; my friends being in a state of inebriety jumped from the boxes in the theatre (eight feet high) on the stage, just before the conclusion of the play, merely to haul down the screen and put the play actors to the rout and confusion. Nothing can excite more diversion to a set of midshipmen than being concerned in those kind of pranks. One of the gentlemen suffered by breaking his leg, which terminated any more frolics that night.

3. Joining the Mediterranean Fleet, December 1798

THE SIGNAL WAS MADE to weigh anchor and we were all obliged to repair on board and bid adieu to England, previous to which I contracted with a bookseller for £15 worth of medical books. These together with the surgeons on board furnished me with a grand library. It was my intention to make great application to my professional study: having 700 men on board, a number of them sick, and the surgeon admired for his surgical skill, I was possessed of good opportunities to improve in my studies. We had very stormy weather, but a speedy passage to Gibraltar. In passing Cabritta Point[14] in Spain, the Spaniards fired a few 32 lb. shot[15] at us. I had very little idea then that at a future period I should be in great jeopardy and have a very narrow escape from the jaws of death at this place. It is a great blessing we do not understand the dangers and accidents that will occur to us in futurity, otherwise we should be continually on the alarm, harassed with anxiety and despair. We ought to admire the profound wisdom of the Divine Being in his excellent arrangements for the welfare of man.

At Gibraltar we procured water and provisions and I had the pleasure of seeing this immense rock. Tremendous by nature and art, the strongest garrison in the world, everything about it will excite curiosity and astonishment. Travellers and antiquarians are highly pleased with its majestic appearance. The antique caverns, subterraneous passages, labyrinths, one cannon placed above another to a prodigious height, the warlike and fortified appearance, give those a sufficient internal satisfaction of its security that have possession of it and a deterrent to its enemies ever to make an attack. Being scanty of cash, my usual misfortune, prevented me from seeing all the curiosities, therefore I contented myself with being involved in deep study all the day, and having my mind relaxed with the adventures of my mess-mates at night.

We sailed to cruise off Cadiz, where Lord Keith[16] left us and went on board the *Barfleur*. The next place we anchored was at Tetuan in Africa. As this was the first time for me to be out of Europe, I was very much surprised with the different aspect of the country. One variety after another excited my curiosity and attention; the more I ruminated, the more I was astonished. We had seven miles to walk to Tetuan. I had a cursory view of the inhabitants as they passed upon jackasses laden with oranges and lemons; their manners and complexion so very different from ours, put me into a state of consternation. As we did not remain long, I was deprived of any further opportunity to make remarks in Africa.

When we arrived down to the beach, two sailors were carrying a young midshipman that was killed by the Moors. Upon inquiry I learned that he had been sent with the party of sailors to procure water, from where he strayed. The Moors that happened to meet him saw he was a beautiful boy and committed their usual and abominable crime of sodomy (they do not conceive it crime and by that means, alas, killed him). The Moors are often guilty of these depredations although allowed as many wives and concubines as they can maintain. As I had a better opportunity to ascertain these facts in other parts of that great quarter of the globe, I will postpone any further account until then.

We returned to our old cruising place, but captured nothing. As our ship, by the Admiralty, was from the first intended for Lord Nelson, we received orders to join him in the *Vanguard* at Naples, at which place we arrived in June 1799.[17] In a few days after our junction his Lordship's flag was hoisted on board our ship. I removed with a few intimate friends on board the *Swiftsure*.[18] I repented this change in a month afterwards: as I was first surgeon's mate on board the admiral's ship, I was entitled to the first vacancy as surgeon and of course going into another ship pro-

longed my promotion. Yet from the following circumstance I blessed the moment I was struck with
the idea. Lord Keith being at that time Commander
& Chief, I was well acquainted with his surgeon, and
through his interest his Lordship gave an order that
I should be sent on board the *Queen Charlotte*, his
flagship, on promotion. When the order came on
board the *Foudroyant*, I was in the *Swiftsure* at
Palermo in Sicily, which prevented me from receiving it for a length of time.

Shortly afterwards the *Queen Charlotte* went to
Leghorn, where by some accident she caught fire
and out of nearly 1000 men, only 40 were saved.[19]
In this dreadful catastrophe I lost the greater part of
my acquaintance. Since this accident I have made
it a point to be reconciled to any change of situation, remarking, although apparently on the contrary, in the end everything will turn out for the
best. Had I remained in the *Foudroyant* one month
longer, I should have joined the *Queen Charlotte*. I
would have been blown up in her and death my
fate; but Providence had ordained that I should
exist longer.

I joined my new ship in the Bay of Naples the 17th
of June 1799. The surgeon received me very politely
and introduced me to my intended messmates, the
greater of whom were old 'Nilors' – in the action of
the Nile with Lord Nelson. There was a scarcity of

provisions as the ship had not time to replenish and was for a short time obliged to live on the King's allowance. Immediately after my junction, we were ordered to Palermo where we had no communication with the shore, except the captain sending dispatches. We returned to the fleet at Naples.

The French had at this time possession of all the strong forts together with the Jacobins or rebels. A body of marines and sailors was sent on shore and me with them as surgeon. When I first received this pleasing intelligence of having an opportunity of going on shore to see this beautiful city, I exulted with joy. I got equipped with instruments, bandages and every other necessary accoutrement in my department for battle.

Our gallant sailors and marines commenced a bombardment and in less than a fortnight the two forts that commanded part of the Bay of Naples surrendered. The rebels after this changed their tune from '*bono Francesco*' to '*bono Ingliso*'. The King of Naples gave orders that all the English officers would form a mess in one of these forts and he would provide them in provisions and every other luxury of life, free of expense, that his kingdom afforded. This mandate came very apropos as it enabled me to live more comfortably, both in body and mind. Living in a high sphere of life and without money were two things that did not act with unanimity. However, I adhered to my old maxim, 'Patience and Perseverance', and consoled myself: in the course of a short time I would be alleviated from all this misfortune.

I lived in the king's castle very comfortably; as I had my provisions gratis, my expenses were trifling. I could always form a very good excuse when any of my comrades asked me to accompany them to routs, balls, ride in a coach etc. etc., that I had a great number of sick and wounded to attend which deprived me of the felicity of their company. Duty was the first thing to be attended to; therefore I begged to be excused.

The barbarities committed at Naples during the rebellion are almost too shocking for me to relate. I shall only give you one as a specimen. On an excursion one night I saw a numerous mob collected, which excited my curiosity and caused me to advance in order that I might be informed of the particulars. The Royalists were putting a traitor under the most excruciating tortures by placing burning sticks to his testicles, consuming him *gradatim*. Two English officers and I liberated him at the risk of our lives.

Our next attack was upon Fort St. Elmo of which the French as yet had possession and commanded part of the town. Captain Hallowell[20] of the *Swiftsure*, with a party of sailors and marines, besieged them in a most gallant manner, after raising a fascine battery contiguous to the castle. We had several men killed and wounded. I was very near to losing my life here. As I was dressing a wounded man, a cannon ball struck a young gentleman on the head, dashing his brains upon all sides; part of them blinded me. At this moment a splinter struck my head and rendered me insensible for quarter of an hour. Upon my recovery, I could hardly persuade myself but what I was mortally wounded, from being completely besmeared with blood and brains. Alas! when I beheld my friend and companion without a head, I could not avoid reflecting with emotions of grief; but the field of battle being no place for weeping or lamentations, with the messengers of death flying around, I contented myself with the usual expression upon the field of battle – poor fellow, there he lies and ends his career.

That night our captain had a gabion battery raised near the fort. The French struck their colours after two days of a brave defence. Shortly after this we marched into the country to take other towns and forts, which we completed without the loss of many men. Our fighting being terminated at Naples and having a number of sick and wounded, I was ordered to continue on shore to dress them.

Naples and its suburbs are remarked for abounding with curiosities and antiquities, but being penniless I had not the means to see them. Shortly after this, I received an account of £20 more of my prize money being due. This pleasing intelligence recruited my spirits and the subsequent day I had a bill drawn on the agent in England. After making reiterated applications to the different merchants at Naples to cash it, I could not succeed. Some said the bill was too small; others had no correspondence in England. I was obliged once more to adhere to my old motto, 'Patience and Perseverance'.

Lord Nelson at last made the signal for officers to repair on board their respective ships. This gave me some internal satisfaction as I should not have so much necessity for money. The whole fleet sailed for Palermo, the capital of Sicily. The King of Naples was all this time on board the *Foudroyant* as he was afraid to trust himself among his rebellious subjects. The king when walking the deck one morning was (and no wonder) astonished to see a late baronet (that he had ordered, and was, hanged until dead) standing with his head and shoulders above the sea. His Majesty was very much frightened. This singular incident caused great consternation through the ship. Upon inquiry they discovered it to be as follows: the rebels, friends to the baronet, did this as a prank, merely to timidate the king. By the means of corks, planks, weights etc. etc. they caused the dead baronet to stand that way in the sea.[21]

We all anchored in line of battle close to Palermo. My first object was to go on shore and obtain cash for my bill. I got the English Consul's address but missed the street. I was now in a complete dilemma, not being capable to find my way or speak one word of their language to ask it. The day being excessively hot, I became greatly fatigued in both body and mind. At length I accosted a friar in Latin[22] who was very civil and affable and accompanied me to all parts of the city I wished, but to my vexation I could not procure cash. I went on board with an intention of not coming on shore again until my purse would be replenished. I occupied my leisure hours in learning that beautiful language, Italian.

The Queen of Naples gave a grand ball and supper at her palace. All the English officers were invited and I accordingly accepted the invitation with great glee as it would be a pleasing variety to dance with and behold the fair Sicilian damsels. The illuminations, decorations, grandeur, music (one hundred musicians) far exceed any praise that I am capable of giving. But when I cast my eyes around and beheld the King and Queen, princes and princesses, marquis and marchionesses, baronets and baronesses, counts, countesses, in short all the nobility of Palermo (none in the mercantile line would be permitted), Lord Nelson and all the English officers in full uniforms made most splendid appearance. The ladies' dresses bespangled with diamonds, gold and silver, their necklaces consisting of a variety of precious stones, some of uncommon brightness, gave a most brilliant and majestic lustre to the assembly.

The charming and delicate complexion of the ladies excited in me the greatest admiration. The island of Sicily has been remarked by all nations to produce some of the most handsome women in all the world. I was introduced by Lady Hamilton,[23] an English lady and wife to Sir William Hamilton who was Plenipotentiary at Naples, to a Sicilian lady and as she spoke a little English, it happened to be a very fortunate circumstance as I had the pleasure of dancing a few country dances and being understood and, of course, passing the night with more satisfaction, and likewise of forming an acquaintance where I might have passed several hours afterwards – which I actually did, but not before I was promoted to surgeon; my present scanty circumstances would not allow me.

The next morning I had the pleasure to accompany my fair *inamorato* home in the coach. I parted with the intention of visiting her again, as customary in this country. It would be considered very impolite not to visit your partner the next evening to enquire after her health. However, upon second consideration this visit would not suit me as I could not do less than to give her coachman and lackey 5s. every time. I sent her a very polite note and begged to be excused as I was suddenly taken ill.

In the evening, after enjoying a few hours of repose, I went with a very intimate friend to the opera. The splendour of the house is almost impossible to describe. I was not a little astonished at the actresses dancing a dance called the bollaro, where they keep a castanet in each hand and chime them with the music. It is performed with that degree of agility you would suppose their feet did not touch the ground. There have been two instances where they have expired from a rupture of a blood vessel in the lungs in consequence of too great an exertion.

My comrade paid all my expenses and as it was too late to get a boat to take us on board, I sallied forth with him wherever he pleased. He was well acquainted with the town and spoke the Italian language. The first place he introduced me into was amongst seven ladies of easy virtue, or vulgarly called prostitutes, where he seemed quite at home. We both supped, and as it was then upon the stroke of one o'clock, we could not procure beds at any inn at such a late hour. I was obliged to remain with one of these damsels all night.

The next morning I went on board with the intention of not coming on shore again, as I was contracting debts and would have no opportunity of paying them, as I should receive no pay until my arrival in England. This is by no means a good custom in Government, not to allow surgeon's mates any pay abroad. On this account, if they make no prize money, they are involved in many pecuniary difficulties. However, there is one advantage – we can not spend it. I am happy to say that they altered this plan the 23rd of January 1806.

We stopped a month at Palermo and sailed again for Naples with the Prince of Naples on board and a large party of his troops to reinforce the Royalists there. On our passage we heard of a French squadron being at sea. We put back again and landed him and all his soldiers. Lord Nelson steered after the French, but unfortunately they got into Toulon. We went to Palermo again where our captain got orders to cruise off Civita Vecchia[24] in Italy, where we remained a considerable time. Nothing of importance occurred, except I had a narrow escape for my life. A French ship was sailing towards the harbour just as we arrived, all the boats were manned, I volunteered my service in the medical line and we set sail after her. We chased her near the harbour's mouth but found it impossible to take her. As soon as we turned back, the French began to discharge their batteries upon us. A 32 lb. shot passed my elbow, carried away a small stick out of my hand, blew the head clean off one man and the body off another. Although the shot was flying very thick, we got on board without any further accident. As we could do nothing with the French here, we left it and went to the island of

Minorca and got water and provisions. After remaining there one month, we received orders to cruise off Cadiz in Spain.

Shortly after our approach to the Spanish shore, a line of battleship and frigates joined us, having obtained a distant hint of a Spanish convoy about to sail from the above port. We cruised with great vigilance for two months, but all to no purpose. The want of water obliged us to go to Gibraltar, where I procured cash for my bill. This terminated all my misfortune in point of money, not having known the want of it since.

We returned off Cadiz and in the course of one week got the authentic intelligence from a Spanish priest that the convoy would soon sail. This account cheered all our spirits and we doubled our activity and vigilance. One evening we saw a sail at a great distance and we chased her for seventy miles close to the Spanish shore. At last she got under their batteries, which caused us, to our great mortification, to give over the chase. The following evening we had the exquisite felicity to see thirteen sail of ships, not the least doubting but what they were the same Spaniards we were so long looking for. The next morning we had the satisfaction to take two of their merchant ships that could not sail as fast as the others. We were rather chagrined that we could not see any more.

The admiral made our signal to chase one way and he took an opposite course. We fell in with nothing that night but had the pleasure to see a ship the next morning, which we chased all day and captured in sight of the Peak of Tenerife. This mountain is situated in one of the Canary Islands in Africa, is two miles and a quarter high and may be seen in a clear day a hundred miles distant. This ship proved to be the very Spaniard we chased for seventy miles before, but to our utmost grief she did not belong to or know anything about the convoy.

In one fortnight we arrived in Gibraltar with our prize in tow. All this time we were under the greatest anxiety whether the admiral took them and even then if we should share for them. Our doubt was soon removed by seeing two fine man-of-war frigates and ten sail of merchants lying in the new mole. Commissioner Englefield,[25] our captain's father in law, came on board before we anchored, knowing we should all be anxious, to announce the admiral thought us entitled to share for our rich prizes valued at £280 to £1000 Sterling. The admiral had fallen in with the whole of the convoy and captured them that evening we left him.

We went again to cruise off Spain where Admiral Sir Richard Bickerton[26] hoisted his flag on board our ship – 1800. After remaining two months, we met with an American ship that had had a desperate engagement, her captain and a great part of the crew wounded.[27] As there was no surgeon on board, I was sent to take care of them until they would arrive in Lisbon, Portugal. Contrary winds caused us to be fifteen days on our passage. We were attacked by a privateer ship of 12 guns. After a gallant defence we got away, but our sails and most every tackle belonging to the ship was cut to pieces. I expected every moment that we should be sunk. I contented myself with making the Frenchman's remark, *'Fortune de la guerre'* (fortune of war).

I had a letter of recommendation from Captain Hallowell to Dr. Harrison, surgeon of the Royal Naval Hospital at Lisbon where I landed all my wounded men. This gentleman received me in the most polite manner that can be expressed. He was very much esteemed in the place amongst the Portuguese. He introduced me to a great number of Portuguese and Irish families, where I passed two months with as much pleasure as ever I did in my life.

I cannot avoid remarking upon a wicked custom amongst the Portuguese, although not consistent with this history: it is bull fighting upon a Sunday. I was promiscuously passing one Sabbath evening when I saw an immense crowd, which induced me to enter and satisfy my curiosity. I saw several men attack a furious bull, using a great deal of art to deceive the animal and at last putting an end to his existence by different kinds of weapons. Horrible is the torment these poor animals suffer. Upon the fall of the bull, whoever has been the most expert receives the loud applause of several thousands of spectators. That evening two men were killed by the animal's horns in consequence of not being expert. In the course of an evening, from twelve to fourteen bulls are killed in this sport. To give a full account of this, it would take several sheets.

The Portuguese – I mean the lower class – are very treacherous; if the least irritated, they will immediately draw their stiletto and stab you. It is requisite for strangers to keep good hours in order to avoid danger. This I adhered to strictly after a sorrowful scene I experienced one night. I went into the country about six miles to spend the evening with a few Irish ladies. Their company was so agreeable that I remained too late and, against all persuasion, I persisted in returning that night to the Naval Hospital. I had a jackass to ride upon, it being very customary for ladies and gentlemen to ride these animals in that place. My ass carried me quietly for three miles, became very fatigued and stubborn and at length lay down and would not move one inch farther. I was in an uninhabited and of course a very lonely place; not a house within three miles in any direction, twelve o'clock at night and, to add to my unpleasant situation, I could see but a very little distance before me.

The more I whipped my ass, the more he hideously groaned and all my stripes were repeated in vain. I began to think of Balaam's ass.[28] I remonstrated with myself whether I was following wickedness, but as my intention was only to go home and loll in the arms of Somnus,[29] I acquitted myself of a clear conscience. Although my ass did not explain himself as well as Balaam's, I will give him that credit, he proved as obstinate.

I was obliged to walk the remainder of the way and, to add to my dreary situation, by a wood. I began to be afraid, not of ghosts or hobgoblins but of thieves. Having no defensive weapon and could not speak their language, in case of an attack by banditti my life would be in a dangerous predicament. Whilst ruminating in this way, I saw at a little distance a man and a horse. I stopped and was afraid to advance any farther. My whole thought was occupied in what manner I should retreat. It would not be prudent for me to return and it was impossible to go off at one side or the other on account of the great forest encompassed with a wall. Upon mature deliberation, I thought best to remain where I was and watch his manoeuvres. Shortly after this I saw a woman with him. My dread began to diminish as I supposed them to be man and wife and probably an accident had happened to them. I advanced closer and on seeing them stoop and apparently in a great bustle, seemed that they were about no good. In ten minutes after this, they mounted their horse and rode off in full speed.

I advance courageously and was in a rage with my own pusillanimity. On my arrival at the spot, to my wonderful consternation, there was a man lying with his throat cut from ear to ear and all his pockets turned inside out. I became tremulous, but as this was of no service to me in my present predicament, I gained all my courage, took two stones in my hand and travelled the rest of the way as fast as possible. I arrived at half past two. When I related the circumstances to my friend Dr. Harrison, he congratulated me on my safe return. He had been in the country a long time and would not take any sum to walk the same road at that hour of the night.

Should you be stabbed in this country, the law can do nothing with the criminal as long as he can get into the Sanctuary or Asylum. The priests protect them there and no one dare take them out. In holy writ they had cities for refuge; in Greece they had an Asylum, but the most famous one was in the Temple of Diana at Ephesus and likewise the Temple of Hercules in Egypt to which bond slaves fled. This privilege originally was not intended to patronise wickedness but as a refuge for the innocent, the injured and oppressed, and in doubtful cases to give men protection until they would have an equitable

hearing. I am sorry to say that these modern sanctu-
aries in Roman Catholic countries are greatly abused
in giving protection to all sorts of criminals. On
account of this protection, more murders are committed there than in England. I have seen and heard
so many in Italy, Sicily, Portugal and Spain that it
would shock me to relate them.

Nothing more particular occurred to me while I
had the felicity to remain at Lisbon, except for
honour's sake I was obliged to fight a duel with a
countryman of my own. He was from the north of
Ireland, had served as an officer in the English Navy
and likewise served to the Germans, Russians and
French, which latter he was obliged to leave at the
time of the revolution. After this, he served in Spain
and left them to come to Portugal to see his mother.
He was a very wild young man, fond of all kinds of
mischievous juvenile frolics. He was detected in some
misdemeanour by a Justice of the Peace, escaped him
and the lash of the law by firing a pistol at the Justice.
Instantaneous death would have been his punishment – even the asylum in this case would not save
him – but being a British subject and having succeeded in getting into the British Hospital, proved,
according to the law, within the walls a place of
safety. We lived in great unanimity until one evening
he became very impertinent. I ordered the steward to
put him out of the gates. The next morning he sent

me a challenge, which I was obliged to accept. We fired one shot at each other but fortunately missed. Dr. Harrison, passing by at the time, interfered; we shook hands and became friends. I was happy at this timely interference as it prevented me from exchanging another shot with an old warrior.

I joined my ship off Cadiz and from the time of our departure from Gibraltar until our return was five months. We were very scarce of provisions and water; the reason of our remaining at sea this length of time was from having gained intelligence of a Spanish galleon[30] expected in Cadiz. As our ship was old, we were surveyed at Gibraltar and supposed not capable to remain out any longer. The pleasant orders at last arrived for us to proceed to England and we immediately put to sea. When we got as far on our passage as Cape St. Vincent, we met Lord Keith with the sea in a manner covered with ships of all description. It was not known then but it turned out afterwards to be upon the Egyptian and ever-memorable expedition.

His Lordship made our signal to return, which caused a gloomy appearance over all our countenances. All our ships, containing from 25,000 to 30,000 soldiers, anchored at a little distance off Cadiz. It now appeared that Lord Keith's intention was to land the army and besiege the town. The Spaniards were panic struck. They sent off a flag of truce and begged the consideration and leniency of our Commander & Chief as the plague was then raging amongst them, hundreds dying and three great destroyers of the human race, fire, pestilence and the sword, would be cruel at the same time. However, all these remonstrances would not do. The soldiers were ordered into the boats and did actually attempt to land, but the wind began to freshen, which caused a great surge on the beach and consequently they could not succeed in landing.[31]

4. The Egyptian Expedition, January 1801

WE PUT TO SEA and anchored in Tetuan Bay on the coast of Barbary to procure water, previous to our going up the Mediterranean. It began to blow in the night tremendously and a great number of our ships broke adrift. Others got foul of each other. We got round Cabritta Point in Spain with great difficulty, drifted back off Gibraltar and lay to all night. The next morning the wind eased. In four days, all our ships collected together again and those ordered to Egypt set sail with a flowing sheet.

Nothing extraordinary occurred until we arrived in Asia Minor. All the convoy anchored in Marmmarise Bay,[32] which is one of the best in all the world and spacious enough to contain the whole British Navy; in that division called Caramania and opposite the island of Rhodes. The commander had a famous opportunity to disciple his troops for a landing in Egypt as we remained here a considerable time to obtain assistance (gun-boats) from our allies the Turks. In the meantime the *Swiftsure* went to cruise and we captured two French ships laden with different articles for the

French army in Egypt. We sent them to our army where they sold the different messes necessaries [*ie* necessities] very well.

As we anchored close to the town of Rhodes, I now had the pleasure of living on shore and taking different routs into the country and beholding a place first peopled by the grandsons of Japhet. Some people are of an opinion that it was by the posterity of Shem who dwelt on the adjacent continent. The apostle Paul touched here on his way to Jerusalem Anno Domini 60. I was not deficient in pecuniary enjoyments, having got £100 prize money before my departure from Gibraltar. In that point I had no constraint upon my desires.

The present inhabitants of this island are mostly Greeks who seemed to me very poor and to be very much oppressed by the Turks, who keep them under great subjugation. I have often reflected on the various changes of the human race that these once flourishing people should allow the Mahomitan race to be their masters: such is the history of Greece.

In all my peregrinations, I have made particular remarks upon the ladies. I had every opportunity of scrutinising them from forming an acquaintance with a Greek gentleman that could speak English. The Greek takes particular care that none of their virgins will be seen for fear her beauty would attract the passionate desires of the Turk, who has it in his power to take her lawfully to his couch by a sentence of the Cadi, or what we call the Judge, and should the virgin show her face willingly, to the Greek it would be considered a great crime, as if an English lady were to show that part she endeavours most to conceal.

There are very few medical men of skill in this country, having no opportunity to learn it. I was called often to see young Greek ladies for a complaint well known to females; all that I have seen, in general, are very handsome, particularly their eyes. At first I did not know they used any artificial means with their eyes but latterly I learned they painted with blue round the eyes and the inside of the sockets with the edges on which the lashes grow tinged with black.

Here stood the famous Colossus, a statue of bronze seventy cubits[33] high, which was once reckoned one of the wonders of the world. A ship with all sail might pass betwixt its legs.

We went over to Marmmarise Bay, but the gunboats would not sail as yet, it being the time of their Ramadan, or of the flight of their Great Prophet Mahomet, a solemn time for fasting, when they neither eat or drink or lie with their wives each day from sunrise until the stars appear. They are so superstitious that they will not wash their mouths or swallow their spittle. They strictly forbid their women to bathe lest water should enter the pudendum. They term this month holy and believe as long as it lasts the gates of paradise are open and hell is shut. The Turks never attempt to fight this month; they would consider it the forerunner of a very unhappy omen and that it would terminate in their fatal destruction.

I went on shore with two of my messmates to learn the manners and customs of the Turks in Asia. Upon our landing I was not a little astonished at the face of the country and the difference between Europe and Africa, which far excels them all in fertility, sweetness, and quality of every specie.[34]

I now began to ruminate in having the pleasure of being in that quarter of the globe where, according to the sacred records, the Divine Being planted the Garden of Eden where the first man and woman were created; and likewise that this quarter became the nursery of the world after the Deluge whence the descendants of Noah dispersed different colonies into other parts of the globe; and it was here where God placed his once chosen people, the Hebrews; but above all, it was here where the great and merciful work of our redemption was completed by his Divine son.

We had three miles to walk up to the village. The first thing that attracted my attention was several camels, buffaloes and dromedaries. I was as much

Camel which I first saw and sketched of with my pencil in Asia, and like all the other sketches, the least friction will obliterate it. I had rough sketches of all the animals I saw abroad, but lost the greatest part of when shipwrecked.

surprised with the animal kingdom as the vegetable. I could not avoid admiring the instinct of the camel kneeling quietly to receive its burden; should they load it too much, the animal will forewarn them by its yells.

The village was very dirty and did not contain a good house. After the walk our appetites began to crave for food but, upon examination, we could not find an appropriate house to regale ourselves. We unanimously agreed to purchase some honey and bread and dine off that. This, together with tobacco, coffee and curious pipes was all this little place afforded. What a pity that those infidels should have the best part of the world when they take no pains to cultivate it. I had not long commenced to suck a honeycomb until two bees that were as much interested to partake of this sweet as myself came and stung me, one upon the lips and the other upon the cheek. A great tumefaction took place, attended with pain. I was quite frightened from having supposed that they might be some inveterate species of wasps, probably similar to the one that stung Queen Cleopatra, which was the cause of her death in Egypt. I had heard of this circumstance a few days before I came on shore and knowing that several of this specie were in the country, I could not avail myself to give over my timid ideas.

This was a kind of serpent that they called the Cerestes[35] or horned viper which Cleopatra employed to procure her death (see Rollin's *Ancient History*) the bite of which is mortal to those that have not the art of guarding against it. Hence the practice of charming alluded to in Psalms 58, Eccles. 10:11 and Jerem. 8:17[36] seems to prevail to this day amongst Turks, particularly in that part of Africa called Egypt, for some of the natives, as I was informed, can play with the Cerestes, which proves perfectly harmless to them that when applied to any other animal they will expire in consequence of the sting.

The governor of Marmmarise satisfied me as to my

mistake, who was a Scotchman, but the renegade, a disgrace to his country, turned Turk, I suppose from gain. He was very civil to us and we were happy to meet with him as we could not understand one word of their language. We went with him to his house; he treated us with a cup of coffee (the custom there). We sat down like tailors upon a mat that was placed upon the floor; the Turks never have any other kind of seat in the house. These mats, as he explained, served them to eat off, sleep and sit. I was soon obliged to rise out of my tailor-like position as my pantaloons were tight and rendered me uneasy.

The Turkish garments are as loose as petticoats and they are accustomed to sit this way from their infancy, and of course can do it with ease. Their chief employment seemed to be smoking from morning until night – yes, and without ceasing – and they have a peculiar way of swallowing the smoke and causing it to come up again and pass through their ears and nose.

He took us out to show us the village. We had not walked much until I saw at a little distance, as I thought, a walking devil. It had neither shape nor human form. I cried with astonishment, what moving lump that was, with two holes in the upper part. The other gentlemen were gazing at the time and the Scotchman told us not to do so as it was a woman and against their laws and regulations to pay the least

*Walking Devil. You can see no more of a Turkish
woman than this when they do, which is very
seldom, walk the street.*

attention on the peril of losing our lives. A woman!
exclaimed they, impossible!

One of them swore, let the consequence be as it
would, he would turn the walking devil inside out
and investigate the contents, drew his sword for the
purpose. The governor cried for the love of God and
their great Prophet Mahomet to cease, otherwise our
heads would be severed from our bodies with their
sabres. Upon our remonstrances this young son of
Neptune sheathed his sword. Now the woman
beholding us for the first time, through the two small
holes in the large robe that covered her from head to
foot, took us as I suppose for devil's imps. She flew
like lightning but in her haste, on entering the door,

stumbled. She bellowed out lustily and in the course of ten minutes there where about a hundred sturdy stout Turks about us. Although we were innocent, they would have killed us only for the timely explanation and interference of the Governor. Indeed, I believe, he could not have saved our lives only they were aware of the consequences that would be the result and the retaliation of the English army, 18,000 men, at a very little distance.

This being amicably settled, my comrades began to interrogate the Governor if there were any ladies of easy virtue. No, answered he, such women here are punished with death and furthermore you may walk the streets to the end of eternity without seeing the face of a Turkish woman, and let me advise you, young gentlemen, not even to look narrowly at them, should any by chance pass you, but above all do not attempt to go into their houses for you may rest assured you will not return with impunity, and perhaps never. The young sons of Neptune did not relish this intelligence, that they should be deprived of female society. They rushed into a hut with their swords drawn and were resolved to see the face of one female at all events. The two women within the hut covered their faces and ran as if attacked by scorpions. This was near terminating in serious consequences: the Turkish commandant made a complaint to Lord Keith; he issued an order that the officers should adhere more strictly to the jurisdiction and not to molest their women or they would answer the contrary upon their peril.

At sunset all the Turks in the street kneeled and prayed with a loud voice to Mahomet; the Governor put himself in the same position. After he performed this service, I asked him why he was so punctual at this hour. Why, sir, said he, the laws of our great prophet are kept very strictly, particularly in washing and praying, which must be performed five times a day. The Turks, not even [*ie* just] here, but in other parts are very strict in following the precepts of Mahomet and before they pray they wash themselves nearly all over.

I sincerely wish that the Christians in general were so punctual in adhering to the precepts of our Blessed Saviour. I am confident from my own remarks that all other nations are more punctual to their own way of worship than Great Britain. A few days subsequent to this, I was passing a mosque. I looked in and saw them praying, kissing the ground and striking their breasts. Curiosity excited me to enter. I took off my hat and one of them made a motion for me to take off my boots and put on my hat. I preferred walking out again. It is as customary with them to take off their slippers on going into the house of worship as it is for us to take off our hats.

I then steered my course to visit the Scotchman (in

order to obtain a further explanation of the manners and customs of the people), who I had learned committed murder which was the cause of him leaving his country and since he had been in Anatolia was guilty of some misdemeanour for which he was mutilated of his nose. He then wore a paper nose which so much resembled the natural one I was a little time in his company before I distinguished it. I made several excursions into the country, which seemed very fertile. They have hardly any trouble in cultivating the ground. They use only one handle to their plough and the bullocks require no driver.

Shortly after this when I was on board the *Swiftsure*, reiterated peals of thunder attended with lightning commenced. The tremendous noise and vivid flashes far exceeded any that ever was heard by the men on board. One flash of lightning struck our mast, split it in pieces and knocked down several men upon the deck. The lightning penetrated as far as the lower deck and consumed several bags. Had it gone a little further it would have set fire to the magazine and blown us up. The tremendous crash frightened us below. I ran up and was very happy to find no other accident had befallen us. The clouds had a most hideous appearance. As soon as I put my head upon deck, I was saluted with hailstones, and every one, to my certain knowledge, was the size of pullets' eggs and, from their specific gravity, fell with an astonishing weight. I began to imagine we should share the same fate as the Amorites when they warred against Gibeon, where God caused so many to be killed with hailstones.[37]

Two days subsequent to this the water rushed down the mountains in such torrents that it carried the trees out of root and everything that opposed it into the valleys. Only for the covenant made by the Lord (the rainbow) I should have taken this to have been the commencement of another Deluge. This violent storm began the 8th of February 1801, which continued two days and two nights. At night the firmament from the repeated flashes was in a continuous state of vivid illumination. The concussion of elements, signal guns of distress heard at the intervals of the thunder ceasing, the howling of wolves and jackals re-echoed through the mountains.

On the 23rd of February we all set sail with a favourable breeze (170 ships) and a numerous set of gun-boats (Turkish). It began to blow very fresh, the Turks were frightened and after bellowing for the assistance of Mahomet, finding their solicitations in vain, put back to the island of Cyprus. We arrived safe off Alexandria on 1st March 1801. We anchored in the very place where Lord Nelson had obtained the glorious victory of the Nile, Aboukir Bay.[38]

The breeze unfortunately began to freshen and consequently from the surging sea it was out of the power of our men to land before the 8th of March. This gave the French sufficient time to collect their forces down to the beach but, fortunately for us, they only brought down 3000 men, supposing that from their advantageous situation, with a number of field pieces, to be enough to prevent the whole British army from landing.[39]

Before daylight all the boats assembled and that night I received my orders from Admiral Bickerton to prepare for going on shore to assist in the medical line as they expected a battle the next morning. I had only three hours to prepare and for the first time got equipped to campaign in a sandy desert:

1[stly]: I had my blanket rolled tight with two broad straps that it might be easy for my shoulders. This was to be my house, bed and lodging.
2[ndly]: a haversack that contained provisions for three days.
3[rdly] : a canteen which held three pints of water.
4[thly]: A calabasse[40] which held half a pint of rum.

This is the way we were are all equipped, whether officers or men.

At nine o'clock the scene of battle began. The French discharged their flying artillery posted on the sand-hills. The great quantity of shells, shot, showers of grape and musketry as thick as hailstones ploughed the water so that apparently it was impossible for any-thing upon it to exist a moment. Several of our flat-bottom boats were sunk (contained fifty men each) before they came near the beach. Those that could swim were picked up by our small boats appropriated for that purpose in the rear. One of my messmates was wounded in the same boat I was in.

Our gallant army landed 5000 men and in a most courageous manner attacked the enemy. The 23rd and 40th Regiments, without firing a shot, rushed up the sand-hills and charged the French battalions with the bayonet and put them all to rout.

The engagement did not last long, but while it con-tinued was very severe and a number killed and wounded on both sides. We had about 700 killed and wounded. The French fled towards Alexandria and before the evening our boats had landed the remain-der of the army. There was a great contrast betwixt the present time and that of our landing, previous to which the impatience and suspense which had agi-tated every mind changed now into the whole army giving three cheers. Expressions of joy were pictured in every man's face from having succeeded in our landing. These cheers were accompanied by several bands of music which animated their spirits to the greatest height.

I was employed about the beach in dressing and stopping the blood of the wounded. On the cessation of the bands of music, my ears were saluted by the lamentations of the wounded and dying. When dressed they were sent back to their ships. That day and night I was incessantly employed. The next day I had more time to view the camp and the parts around.

Every small valley was filled with human bones. I now remembered the prophecy of Ezekiel Chap. 37, particularly verse 2nd: 'And caused me to pass by them round about; and, behold, there were very many in the open valley; and, Lo, they were very dry'. He prophesied, but I had ocular demonstration. The French had killed 30,000 of the Turks in a desperate battle. They were buried here after the contest and in the course of time the wind blew the sand off the graves and consequently they became exposed.

Our army marched one mile towards Alexandria, where they encamped. Nothing particular occurred until the 13th of March, previous to which we got our haversacks reinforced with provisions from the ships. The French had by this time collected all their forces from Grand Cairo, Rosetta, Alexandria, etc. etc. which amounted to 13,000 men. Our battalion of marines (1000 men) was landed and placed in the left wing of the army. The day before the 13th, I was attached to them. That night all our troops were anxious for the break of day, knowing at that time a battle would begin from our out-scouts ascertaining the enemy's position and having a few skirmishes occasionally.

As soon as the dawn appeared, the two armies met in a most courageous intrepid manner. There was hardly a word spoken by ours and not the least noise except from marching. Our sailors were obliged, from the want of horses, to draw the artillery through the deep burning sands, where the French had from six to eight horses in each field piece. When the engagement commenced, the scene was soon changed: the din of arms, tremendous and reiterated noise of the cannons, the whizzing of the shot, the whole plain covered with smoke. In a short time the French army was obliged to retreat. This, of course, was encouragement for our men, who followed them up with undaunted spirit.

I was employed in dressing the wounded in the rear. In a short time, from our army advancing, I was out of reach of musketry, for which I was not the least sorry; but the cannon shot annoyed me a little, flying about in all directions. The battle continued until night; we drove the enemy under the walls of Alexandria, who were forced to retreat thirteen miles after making every obstinate defence in their power.[41]

We dressed the wounded French as they had not time to bury or take them with them, which they in general do in order to deceive their enemy of the number slain. This was plainly perceived by them leaving at times in their haste a foot or a hand of their slain uncovered, from the rapid advancement of our army.

Being a young campaigner, I gave the greater part of my water to the wounded, who cried for God's sake to give them a drop to drink to keep them from dying. Towards the night I reflected on my past conduct as I was prodigiously thirsty and no water to be procured. The French filled all the wells and we had not time as yet to search for them. I now began to be very fatigued and my blanket and provisions, although seemed light at first, began to hang on my shoulders like as much lead. This day we had 1500 men killed and wounded. We suffered the most in this battle because the French had every advantage of us, being well accustomed and acquainted to every track of ground. At dark I joined my regiment, which had retreated from the range of the enemy's shot under the walls of Alexandria.

In Egypt the day is extremely hot and the sun very penetrating as even to scorch the skin off our faces. The nose in particular suffered. The reflection of the sun from the ardent sand, to those not accustomed, was very destructive to the eyes. A great number of our men lost their eyesight entirely from this cause. The inhabitants bake eggs in the sand – it would be almost impossible in the heat of the day to keep your bare feet one moment on the sand. The night was on the other extreme, both chilly and cold, which caused the flux to be so prevalent in our camp.

All our army encamped on a small hill opposite to the enemy. A man, cool and collected, to walk these thirteen miles after the battle, to see the wounded dying and dead, both human and brutes, some cut in twain, others with their heads knocked off, to hear their weepings and lamentations, must be often agitated with horror and grief. It was astonishing to see the wounded horses bear their pain with so much fortitude. However, I made it a point, when I met any of these animals, to put them out of pain by firing a pistol ball through their heads.

From my remarks the French in general bear their wounds and misfortunes with more fortitude than the English. I dressed a French officer on the 13th of March who had one arm shot off, his cheek cut and fifteen lesser wounds on various part of his body. He seemed to take it as easy as if nothing ailed him. I saw him afterwards when quite well. He expressed his gratitude with the greatest degree of cordiality and proved to be a particular friend of mine when I was a prisoner in Toulon.

The battalion of marines two days after this received orders to march to the Aboukir Castle, about thirteen miles distant, to besiege it. We commenced our march at sunset, preferring that time to the heat of the day. We went seven miles that night where we arrived amongst a number of date trees. We set the men to work to make huts to shelter us from the night dews. The Almighty has ordained everything for the best and the more we explore distant climates, the more we ought to admire the profound wisdom of our Great Creator. The branches of these date trees are very broad and spreading. Two men in the course of one hour will make a comfortable hut by raising the sand all round and sticking and entangling the branches. Those are the kind of huts that the wandering tribes of Arabs erect and from habit make themselves as happy as the first nobleman in his palace.

These trees grow in great abundance in some parts of Egypt and, what is very singular, grow in couples, male and female. The female is not fruitful without growing beside the male and having his seed mixed with hers. The nature of this tree is that it will resist any weights put upon it; for this reason it was placed in churchyards in Eastern countries as an excellent emblem of resurrection. After supper we put a candle in the middle of our little temporary fabrication. Just as I was about to sleep, I saw a centipede, an ugly creature with a hundred feet, from whence its name, creeping upon my blanket. This being a poisonous insect, I dreaded the idea of sleeping that night.

Shortly after this, a quantity of sand fell on one of our officers' head that was asleep. Had he been alone he would have been smothered. In addition, to our

Lost the sketch of the Centipede
Ichneumon or the rat of Pharaoh just caught this
serpent and prevented my night's repose

surprise, a dead soldier with his entrails hanging out came tumbling afterwards. As he had been buried in the action of the 13th, an uncommon stench proceeded from his body, which completely routed us out of our lodgings. As the other huts were filled, we were obliged to choose a place exposed to the dews among the date trees. From seeing a large snake and hearing strange yells that I never had been accustomed to before entirely interrupted my night's repose, although very much fatigued.

We had seven miles to march the next morning. I would rather walk thirty in England on account of the ardent sun and sand, the reflection of the former upon the latter and our feet sinking a considerable way at each step. About the middle of the day we arrived near Aboukir Castle and encamped behind a hillock to be in readiness to attack about a hundred French who still kept possession of this castle. All that day we employed the drummers and fifers to erect huts, as is customary in the army for these musicians to assist the surgeon and his assistants on all occasions.

In two days time we became more settled and comfortable, being supplied with provisions and spirits from the ships, and camp kettles to boil it, before which we were obliged to eat our salt pork raw. At first it did not agree with my organs of digestion, but latterly tolerably well. This clearly demonstrates that we may habituate ourselves to any fare we please.

But one morning whilst enjoying our breakfast, the French, having discovered our position, fired a few shot in our direction, one of which struck our hut and unfortunately knocked the head off one marine soldier and the shoulder off another while in the very act of putting a morsel into their mouths. The colonel, our commander, gave us orders to march out of the range of the shot. The enemy, perceiving our movements, fired at us whilst marching to three quarters of a mile. The most brave, at the time, could not avoid to be a little dispirited at the shot whizzing around, and the whole plain being covered with human bones.

On the 19th of March I received orders to proceed to the Grand Army. I was obliged to travel in the heat of the day. The reflection of the sun was so powerful that at times I was almost deprived of sight, which I recovered by holding my hand upon my eyes or sitting down under the shade of a date tree where I had the good luck to meet with any. I arrived at the Grand Army a little before sunset and regaled myself on my usual fare: salt pork, biscuit and rum. I took particular care to have a good supply of the latter, having got an advice from an old campaigner to take a mouthful during the night if I should be chilly, which might be the means of preventing the flux.[42]

Nothing very material occurred until the 21st of March when we had the grand and ever memorable battle where our noble Commander-in-Chief fell, Sir Ralph Abercrombie.[43] The French attacked us before daylight in the morning, after receiving orders to drive us all into the sea, which was as much as to say, give them no quarters. However, they met with so gallant and spirited defence, they were obligated to retreat after a most obstinate and bloody conflict of six hours, but not before they left on the field of battle 4000 of their countrymen killed and wounded. Here we gained a complete victory over our enemies. The tents were almost torn to pieces by the shot and several servants killed in the inside. The sick in a most miraculous manner escaped.

We had 1000 killed and wounded. The wounded were so numerous that it was impossible for the medical gentlemen to render them all assistance in good time. We took care to dress our own men first but alas! a number of the French died for want of surgical assistance, poor fellows, nothing even to cover them from the scorching sun. A man now to behold 5000 men, 500 horses, camels, etc. etc. lying in such a small compass on the field of battle, and give himself a few moments to reflect upon the horror of war, alas! what must his feelings be at the present moment to see so many of his fellow creatures slain and weltering in human gore, to hear the lamentations and weeping of the wounded and dying. He must utterly detest the very thought of war and sincerely wish that nations could agree in unity and concord to prevent so much human slaughter and the tears of their friends and relations to flow in torrents round the land.

In four days after this desperate contest we got all the sick removed to hospital tents where they were more commodious and better attended. The Arabs brought a great quantity of sheep and poultry of all kinds from the land of Goshen,[44] which not only supplied the sick but the whole army, very cheap and in good order. You might purchase a sheep from 3s. to

5s. and every other thing in proportion. From all accounts, this land has been famous for cattle ever since Jacob dwelt there.

Shortly after this I went to Civitas Heroum in Goshen, a small village, which is so remarkable, where Joseph had the first interview in his chariot with Israel his father.[45] The village now is in ruins. It was from Rameses in this land where the children of Israel took their departure. My next rout was to Grand Cairo, but had not the pleasure of entering that city as the French had as yet possession of it.

The plague at this time was raging in some parts of Egypt. The Turks are a very slovenly set and take no trouble to keep their places clean, in consequence of which they have the plague amongst them, which often cuts off thousands. They credit predestination and are so superstitious that they will not use, and would think it a heinous crime to use the least preventative against this raging malady. Not being allowed to remain long here, I had not much time to make many remarks. The city was built on the ruins of Babylon Aegyptorum.[46]

I was sorry for leaving this so soon as it was my intention, with a few other officers, after the surrender of Cairo, to visit Suez (the ancient arsenal) about sixty-six miles distant from where we were. We might have gone up by water and, what made it still more desirable to be seen, it is affirmed to be the dwelling place of Joseph and Mary when they fled with Christ from the fury of Herod. I was informed by several travellers that a great number of aged Christian Cophts[47] resorted to this town in order to die there. History informs us that Cyrene Simon was born there who the Jews compelled to carry our Blessed Saviour's cross.

My eyes became inflamed. I was ordered back to Rosetta.[48] I had a short opportunity to see the Pyramids. They are, indeed, most tremendous and stupendous fabrications. History relates that 36,600 men were employed for twenty years to erect the largest. Its base covers from ten to twelve acres of ground. The stones are of an immense size, no stone so small as to be drawn by any of our carts. The Labyrinth that is situated on the bank of the Nile is another amazing construction; strangers will lose their way if they do not take care.

On my arrival at Rosetta my eyes became better. This place, from its verdure, was more grateful to the sight. The land where the river Nile overflows is the most fertile in all the world. At all events it requires the least trouble to cultivate it; it does not require more trouble than to sow the seed. One of the Arabs informed me that should the Nile not overflow its banks, it would cause famine. He was old and it happened once in his life.

It is mentioned by creditable authors, in the tenth

and eleventh years of the reign of the beautiful Queen Cleopatra, that the river did not increase, which proved an omen to the fall of her and her sweet Antonius. But what is more singular, a contagious malady sometimes rises a few days before the flood and destroys hundreds. Immediately after the flood the disease ceases. It appears from this that the health of the inhabitants, purification of the atmosphere, and the land producing abundance, depends on the overflowing of this river.

For the first time since my landing in Egypt I got under the roof of a house, but pleasure and pain is so blended together it is very difficult to have the one without being succeeded by the other. That night I lay down in the arms of Somnus with an intention of enjoying a sweet repose and relax my wearied limbs after so much fatigue, but soon found myself deceived from being attacked in all quarters by little gnats, called Musquitos. They lie very quiet all day but on the approach of night, make a great noise, creep under your blankets and sting you all over. When I arose in the morning, I was very much surprised to see red painful swellings over the major part of my body. I procured a looking glass and when I looked in it, I started back, from the tumefaction of my face. My complexion changed by the scorching sun, I was surprised at my own figure and could hardly be convinced but that I was transformed into an Arabian; but as my rational ideas got the better of my ocular speculations, I was soon convinced that I was still an Irishman. Those annoying insects are very numerous in all hot climates. In the Christian countries they use Musquito curtains which prevent their entrance.

The blind are numerous here, nearly every sixth inhabitant has lost or has some bad humour in his eyes. The dropsy, leprosy, erysipelas, elephantiasis and wonderful contortions are very disagreeable to the sight.

When the castle of St. Julian surrendered to the English shortly after the surrender of Rosetta, a number of black and French young women were found in the fort. The black women were offered for sale and some very nice women were bought for 5s. I say nice women because it was a great treat even to behold a woman. A handsome face, with a white straw hat ornamented with flowers, was an agreeable sight, where we had before seen none except those monsters or walking devils as mentioned before.

An officer asking the price of a black woman, the word Espagnol was mentioned, which means a Spanish dollar (value 5s.). She gave a dreadful yell on hearing that word. I suppose it had been used for her sale before, which no doubt put her in mind of a second barter. At the camp before Alexandria five sailors joined and bought a woman from the Arabs for seven dollars. During the auction she cried heartily, but after her lot was terminated, she submitted to be led by a halter to the lake, where she was stripped naked, scrubbed clean and taken off to the ship.

Before I left here, I had the pleasure to see eleven Arab chiefs of grand appearance, but the men who accompanied them were ill looking fellows and badly dressed with a pair of loose linen pantaloons and coarse blanket thrown round them with a hood. No person, to behold these chiefs, could avoid remembering the Patriarchs Abraham, Isaac and Jacob, for no improvement has ever been made amongst these tribes ever since, but on the contrary, a corruption of morality.

The next orders I received was to repair to where the marines were encamped, who had got tents which defended them from the dews, but the greater part were sick. I had not remained there one day until I was attacked with the flux, but fortunately for me my friend Admiral Bickerton, on hearing this, ordered me on board, as I should be better attended and recover sooner. If I was anxious to get on shore, I was doubly so to go on board my own ship as I was completely tired of campaigning. I was six weeks harassed by this complaint and reduced to a mere skeleton, but thank God I soon retrieved from a debilitated and emaciated state.

Before I left Egypt I had the pleasure to see the small island of Pharos situated opposite to Alexandria. From the height and size of its lighthouse it was anciently considered one of the wonders of the world, but it is at present greatly reduced. This island is remarkable for being the place were the Septuagint translation of the Bible took place. As history informs us, Ptolemy Philadelphus, having erected a very large library at Alexandria containing 700,000 volumes, being desirous to have the Bible as an addition, he obtained liberty from the Jewish high-priest to have it translated from Hebrew into Greek. Seventy-two elders were appointed and sent upon this island.[49]

Philo tells us that each of them translated the whole Bible separately and yet there was not the least difference, either in sense or expression, between their several translations. He concluded from this they were all directed by the Spirit of God. Justin Martyr and other Fathers assure us that they worked in separate cells and had no communication with each other, but their translations were found to be uniform and agreeable. The learned Dr. Prideaux has fully treated this subject. The Septuagint translation (differs) exceeds the Hebrew Bible 606 years from the Deluge to the birth of our Saviour.[50]

5. Prisoner of War, June 1801

OUR SHIP BEING OLD, it was unanimously agreed by the carpenters she was not in a fit state to remain abroad another winter and consequently was ordered home. Admiral Sir Richd Bickerton, a particular friend of mine and very much interested in my welfare and promotion, gave me my choice to go on board Lord Keith's ship with a letter of recommendation from him to his Lordship, or to go to England in the *Swiftsure* and he would give me a letter to the Commissioners for taking Care of Sick and Wounded Seamen and Marines. After an hour's consideration I adopted the latter on account I might have an opportunity of seeing my relations. The Turkish admiral came on board to bid adieu to our captain. His retinue was very splendid. His pipes that he smoked out of would be a handsome fortune which they always take with them as they smoke the greater part of the day. The shanks of their pipes, two yards in length, were set all over with diamonds.

The long wished for time arrived with a favourable breeze for England. As our crew had been a long time on a foreign station, they received this intelligence with the greatest cordiality, and expressions of joy were painted on every man's face. Four miles from Egypt our decks were covered over with fine sand which the wind blew off the coast that wonderful length – hence it is no wonder that whole caravans when travelling to India are buried by the sands. Alas! what must the spectator imagine when he beholds a mountain of sand coming before the wind, in a short time to be overwhelmed in it. Thousands have met with this fate.

It will not be much amiss to assert a few remarks by Captain Dunkan here, although in some degree digressing (which I wish to avoid as much as possible) from the history of my own life. There are several sorts of caravans, the heavy, light and common, etc. etc. The former consists of 500 elephants, 2000 horse and 1000 dromedaries. Each elephant (see page 148) carries two soldiers and a young lad whose business is to prick the animal forward with a sharp pointed iron. Although they consist of such enormous bodies, they are often attacked by the freebooting Arabian princes and make them captives.

Innumerable are the disappointments to which a merchant submits who enters into this mode of travelling, since the whole body, en masse, are subject to be lost in the horrid boundless tracks of parched deserts where neither vegetation or water bless the soil, where clouds of moving dust, deep burning and of an extent of many miles, sometimes bury whole caravans under one trackless grave. Should the guide lose his way and the water fail, all must wander till they perish from thirst and fatigue. Dreadful too is the scene when the south wind blows upon the caravan. The Arabs call it poisonous and the only means of escape for the wretched travellers is to cover their mouths with a linen cloth and hide their faces in the burning sand until this tremendous wind be passed lest they swallow instantaneous death.

On our passage we received intelligence from the *Pigmy*[51] that a French squadron had been seen about two days ago, in consequence of which we hauled our wind close to the Barbary shore[52] with an idea to escape them. But as they had acted on the same principle to escape the English, unfortunately for us, three days afterwards at daylight we saw four sail of the line and a frigate. We consoled ourselves by concluding that it was an English squadron. When daylight was more advanced that their signals could be distinguished, we were disagreeably deceived in discovering them to be French.

They chased us from the dawn of day until four o'clock in the evening, at which time two of their ships came up within a pistol shot and fired a great gun, which we returned with a whole broadside. We continued a very severe and desperate battle for a long time against double our force. After our masts, yards and rigging were all cut to pieces, a number of our men killed and wounded, the other two ships within shot of us, upon a consultation, the captain, officers and men agreed to strike to the enemy in order to prevent any further slaughter which would be attended with no advantage to our country. At this time we saw the island of Candia and it was our captain's intention to have run his ship upon it and set fire to her provided the enemy had not come up so soon.[53]

Now the contrast was very great between our receiving orders to proceed to England and surrendering ourselves prisoners of war. Every man became melancholy and sorrow was pictured on their countenance – no wonder when the major part of them had been out of their country for eight years and on a fair way to beholding their wives, friends and relations. These pleasing ideas had exhilarated their spirits to the greatest height, where on the other extreme the idea of going into a French prison was sufficient to depress them for a time with every degree of gloomy sadness. In the course of an hour we had on board 700 Frenchmen.

The time I was attending the wounded, some of them stole from me a trunk of clothes. Two French sailors were found in the fact and punished. In order that these desperate fellows would have revenge, they went privately to the magazine and set a lighted candle in a cask of powder to blow us up, but they were again found out by a sentry, who took the candle out of the cask. What a lamentable catastrophe had they succeeded in their horrible plan that 700 Frenchmen, 70 English sailors and all the officers belonging to His Majesty's late ship *Swiftsure* would have lost their lives by the revenge of two individuals. Our time to leave this world had not arrived and profound thanks ought to be returned to the Divine Being for His mercies in not allowing us to be called away before we would have a moment of repentance.

This French squadron had 4000 troops on board. They had made several attempts to land in Egypt and were a long time at sea. Consequently, every man was on an allowance of water. Before we surrendered, we had only a fortnight's water on board and were therefore obliged to live on the proportion of a pint of water and half a pint of wine per diem with a little salt pork and biscuit. I sincerely wish it to be the last – no man can have the least idea of that insufferable punishment, thirst, but those who have once experienced it. To add more to our misery, the wind was not favourable to send us into a French port. Patience and suffering were our only resource. We had no reason to complain, having the same allowance as the French. Latterly I was more comfortable, having contracted with a French sailor that stole a bottle of water per day and sold it to me at 3s. a bottle.

When we arrived within thirty miles of the coast of France, a very serious accident occurred. A hogshead of rum took fire in the cockpit close to the magazine of powder, which put us all on a great alarm. In place of the French sailors exerting themselves to extinguish the flames, they all ran forward and a great number jumped overboard. At this instant I came on the quarterdeck and when I looked down the hatchway I was nearly suffocated with the fumes. The French admiral's ship, that had us in tow, cast us off. The flame increasing and no assistance rendered, I thought it full time to prepare to jump into the water; out of two evils let us choose the least. My mind was very much agitated, expecting every moment to have been blown up. I hauled off my boots to be more enabled to swim and went again to see if the fire was increasing. Shortly and fortunately after this, one English officer and eight of our sailors cut several hammocks down and smothered it. The French admiral rewarded each with one guinea. The French have very bad discipline amongst their men: hence the superiority of our fleet at sea. The men are very dirty, the smell not of the most fragrant kind.

It was three weeks from the time we were captured until our arrival in Toulon,[54] and I must confess, although an enemy's port, it proved to be as happy a moment as ever occurred to me in my life; being stinted with both meat and drink, did not agree with my organs of digestion. We bought a sheep and prepared the one half among four of us and feasted heartily. In a short time we drowned all our sorrows in a few bumpers of French wine.

My next orders was to repair on board a French hulk to visit seventy English sailors, ill of the yellow fever. The French surgeon, who had been a long time prisoner in England, spoke good English and received me with the greatest friendship and cordiality, made me live with him and obtained a servant for me. He did everything in his power to make me happy, even offered me money, took me with him to all parties of pleasure. Indeed, all the officers behaved with great civility and attention. Although we fight desperately against each other, after surrendering we act more like brothers. All animosity subsides, and very properly: why should individuals remain any longer enemies (after the fulfilment of their duty) for the ambitions of kings and princes?

I remained one month at Toulon, at which time an exchange of prisoners took place and we all went in a cartel to the island of a Minorca.[55] I was very anxious to proceed from Minorca to England. The captain had obtained liberty from the admiral, but shortly after this a vacancy for a surgeon occurred, which proved to be a very fortunate circumstance for me. I was appointed surgeon to the *Pigmy*, Anno 1801, and found myself very comfortable on my promotion and new situation. Our commander was ordered to Egypt with dispatches, which I did not relish; I had a natural antipathy against that place ever since my last campaigning.

We arrived and anchored off Jaffa,[56] anciently called Joppa, and sent dispatches from there to Egypt. This is the place where Bonaparte, after storming this town, marched out, of the miserable inhabitants that had surrendered, 4400 men, about a mile in the way towards Gaza and in cool blood put them all to death. I have seen the skeletons of those unfortunate victims which lie spread over hills etc. etc. The houses of Jaffa are very little and are surrounded by ancient walls and towers. Pilgrims are obliged to pay for permission to visit the holy city Jerusalem.

Being only thirty-seven miles from the city, my mind was continually agitated until I gained permission with another officer to visit Jerusalem. We procured guides, camels and provisions, set off before daylight and arrived there before dark, where we dismissed our Janazaries[57] as there is always kept in the city a number of these soldiers to protect the multitude of Christian pilgrims that flock from various parts of the world from the insults of the Arabs. History informs us that the Emperor Adrian built a new city near where the ancient Jerusalem stood. It now stands upon a high hill or rock with ascents around. The place adjoining Mount Calvary called Golgotha, where our Blessed Saviour suffered without the gates, is now nearly in the centre of the city. Mount Sion is excluded.

We went next up Mount Olives (it may well be called so, it produces a great number of these fruits which I am fond of) where we had an excellent prospect of Jerusalem. When our Saviour was on this Mount, notwithstanding the small distance, it might be remarked in a literal sense that he wept over it. I have often wondered why the Turks call this city Heleodes, which signifies the Holy City, after their disbelief and aversion to the Christian religion.

They have erected on Mount Calvary a large structure something similar to a pantheon, which has no light but what comes through the top. This is called the Church of the Holy Sepulchre. After passing three days in and around Jerusalem, we agreed to proceed to Bethlehem in Judea, about six miles from Jerusalem, to behold the place where our Blessed Saviour was born, which is situated on a ridge of a hill; a miserable looking place and contains a few poor Greeks. They have a convent with a door that opens into the holy manger, which is always showed to the pilgrims who in general resort thither before they leave the land of Canaan.

We bought a great quantity of wine here for a mere trifle. I met with several Roman Catholic priests of

Spain and Portugal on the Mount of Olives who came on purpose to make crucifixes and necklaces out of the branches of the olive trees. They consecrate them in the Holy Sepulchre and when they take them to their respective places, distribute them to the Catholics who are very anxious and consider it a blessing conferred upon them to receive them. The last prize we took in the *Weazle* at the commencement of this war was from Aleppo and had on board seven priests and seven immense chests full of these consecrated crucifixes and beads, which we allowed them to take home.

No sight ever pleased me so well as that of Palestine or gave me more gratification. It only cost me £20 expenses altogether, where those that set out from England with an intention of seeing it, an immense sum.

We steered from this to the island of Candia, the ancient Crete and called also Hecatompolis from its one hundred cities.[58] Here I had an opportunity of seeing the river Lethe and Mount Ida, for an account of which see the Latin authors. We got water and provisions. After cruising a short time, the next place we put into was Ephesus,[59] anciently the celebrated city of Ionia, famous for the temple of Diana, one or two columns of which remain to this day, supposed to be part of it. The inhabitants, who are Greeks, are very illiterate and ignorant, and I am confident do not understand that fine Epistle which St. Paul wrote to them; alas! what human degeneracy.

We from thence sailed to the island of Elba. The French had possession of the whole except the city, which was so well fortified it was impossible for them to take it. Admiral Sir Jn° Bolus Warren had a small squadron there. He ordered a party of sailors and marines to land and rout them out of the island. We were obliged to land in the very mouth of the enemy, but made good our landing, took two batteries and spiked their guns. This country abounding in wines, our sailors, to their shame, got intoxicated and upon a second battle with the French a great number of our men were killed and wounded or made prisoners. Those that were nearest the beach retreated precipitously into the boats and shoved off. I fortunately happened to be amongst this number and I congratulated myself as usual that I had escaped from the jaws of death.

We were ordered to cruise between Elba and Italy and sometimes to stretch out as far as the island of Corsica to intercept the French from reinforcing their troops in Elba. We had not cruised one month until we fell in with a ship from Genoa. After a chase of twelve hours we arrived within gunshot, when it became calm. She got her stern guns to bear upon us and made a running fight for three hours, cut our rigging very much and wounded several of our men.

The breeze freshened and as soon as we got our broadside to bear, poured the contents of our nine guns – each shot weighed 18 lbs – put our ship about and gave her the same quantity from the other side, when she surrendered. In three days we sold her; I received fifty guineas prize money.

I used to make several excursions into the town of Elba, but we had some difficulty, at least danger, in passing the batteries in the boat, as the French were firing at us. They had besieged the town for a long time and had nearly knocked down all the houses by throwing in shells. What a lamentable catastrophe to see men, women and children collected in groups and half starved under the bomb-proofs,[60] weeping, wailing and gnashing of teeth. Innocent babies hanging on their mothers' bosoms seemed quite sensible of their hard fate, wives exhausted, crying and looking to their husbands for protection which was not to be found at this critical moment, husbands sunk to the earth in despondency and despair from beholding their houses levelled to the ground where they had enjoyed all the blessings of a domestic life, surrounded and rendered happy by the complacent smiles of their little ones; but alas! now the scene was changed, yes, cruelly changed by not only being deprived of their all but their families rendered miserable from the horror and consequences of war.

We walked a long way under the bomb-proofs

from one lamentable scene alternating with another, the air not very pure or the smell of the most fragrant kind, making my exit very pleasing. The commander having delivered the dispatches to the governor, we were obliged to take the same route again. When passing through the shattered houses, the French began to throw their shells very quickly. One fell and burst near us; we narrowly escaped by lying flat.

We went to the same place to cruise, had several skirmishes but not worth mentioning. We captured another prize in a most gallant manner under the French batteries after a very severe conflict in a dark night, for which two other ships laid in their claim. We had a lawsuit and gained our point, only we had to pay 1000 dollars towards the expenses.

From this we proceeded to Sardinia to cut wood and get water. I was highly entertained in going amongst the woods to shoot wild bullocks, goats and sheep, which place abounds with them. We stopped for a fortnight and I had an opportunity to mix with the inhabitants. In all foreign countries they are remarkably civil and polite to English officers. We always had a succession of invitations, but they are a poor, indolent set of beings. Their soldiers are half starved, their pay not being sufficient to support them.

The scene has now changed from hard fighting to luxury and ease. My mind was very much relaxed in going to their dances and hearing their music, yet at times a little agitated from not being capable to enter into the spirit of conversation with the Sardinian damsels. I was just then beginning to chatter a little Italian.

We then steered to our old cruising place, when we received the intelligence of peace from a French brig between Great Britain and France.[61] According to the political agreement, we were allowed six weeks to capture vessels and, of course, it was our interest to cruise with vigilance and we captured another prize.

6. Peacetime Pursuits, 1802

ON MY LANDING AGAIN in Elba, I had the infinite felicity to behold the miserable scenes changed into mirth
and jollity from the cessation of hostile arms. When
our time expired, we sailed to Civita Vecchia, a
seaport town in Italy thirty-five miles from Rome.
Our commander having a numerous acquaintance
here, and being peace, we were highly entertained in
every diversion and luxury of life.

It is a singular and very gratifying custom to
behold the wild boar hunting. This country abounds
with these savage animals. A number of gentlemen,
and sometimes ladies, mounted on horses with spears
in their hands makes a very splendid majestic
appearance. They surround a wood and the instant
the animal appears, they set off in full chase. The first
that kills the wild boar, which is attended with great
danger and at times lives lost upon the occasion,
receives reiterated applause and exclamations of
approbation for their valour. The sight of this animal
with open mouth, tusks a foot long, was sufficient to
deter a stranger to this sport from any attempt. I was
introduced to a number of respectable families by the

English consul and as no other language was spoken but Italian, I was always improving.

I have often been amazed at the immodesty of some of the Italian females comparatively with ours. When walking with them, they did not use the least ceremony in hauling up their petticoats and exposing half of their thigh to tie their garter, in case their stocking would accidentally fall down; custom of the country had rendered this as well as other things practically, and of course not so immodest as strangers would suggest at first sight. On our arrival indoors, the first thing that the ladies would call for was a small pot containing a few clear burning coals which they immediately popped under there petti-coats to keep their thighs warm and those parts con-tiguous. This being in winter, I do not deny that the custom is beneficial in point of warmth but very prej-udicial in other respects by causing a great relaxation and subjects them to a disease which is very incident to the fair sex.

The commander and I embraced this opportunity to go and see Rome, but as we could only stop there three days, we had little time to investigate this ancient city. We were employed the most part of the time in viewing St. Peters Church, which is larger and more splendid than St. Pauls in London. We are informed that the building of St. Peters was the work of a hundred years and cost 40 millions of Crowns,

5s.-6s. each. They say that under the altar half the
bodies of St. Peter and St. Paul are deposited;
upward of one hundred lamps are continually
burning before it. I have been in several Catholic
churches in Italy and one at Malta where they
pretend to have some of the relics of St. Paul
deposited. I believed this at first on hearing it from
the Reverend Fathers but I know from experience
that it is priestcraft as they presumed to have in the
church of Malta and one in Italy the bones of the right
leg of that saint. It is well known that they did not
walk on three legs in those days.

We came down that beautiful river Tiber to join
our ship and then set sail for the island of Minorca.
The women at Minorca continue a very ancient and
curious custom of wearing black petticoats, short
gowns but long waists, hair of the head plaited and
hanging down to the under part of their petticoat.
Altogether they appear a singular figure to strangers.
Their method of dancing excited me to a great fit of
laughter. In place of moving their feet, they stand
after turning the corners and wriggle all parts with
the music, which makes it a very lewd spectacle and,
to those not accustomed, lascivious ideas.

At this island I had a narrow escape for my life.
The commander of the *Pigmy* was fond of a woman
that kept a pretty inn and we resorted thither in plain
clothes to drink a bottle of wine. The captain of a

merchant ship with his mate intruded into our room. We requested them civilly to abscond out of our apartments and upon their flat denial, we called the woman to prove our rights. As they still persisted and both parties being intoxicated, my companion began to fight with the mate and we drove them out upon the street. I never enjoyed more diversion than I did in that first part but when the captain began to interfere I was obliged likewise. He pulled out his small sword and made a lunge at my body, which I luckily fended off. This blood-thirsty attempt giving me additional courage, I ran at him like a furious tiger, broke his sword, caught him by the throat and would have completely choked him, as his face was swollen and his tongue out of his mouth, only for the timely interference of a third person.

At this time our boat's crew came for us; thus our antagonists understood we belonged to a man of war and were very frightened. However, it was then too late. I left the commander in quiet possession of the room and lady which we obtained by victory. I then proceeded on board with our two prisoners; they were put in irons. After a solemn repentance of their past conduct, they were allowed to go to their own ship.

We sailed from this to the island of Malta, called in the Scriptures Melita, were I was superseded per order of Lord Keith and appointed to His Majesty's

Sloop *Weazle*[62] in Anno 1802. I remained a long time here, which gave me an opportunity to explore this ancient island, particularly as St. Paul was ship-wrecked at this place. My first excursion was to see the rock where St. Paul's ship struck and the Reverend Fathers assert it to be the very place and showed me that part which seemed to be struck with a stem of a ship.[63] Whether true or not I cannot confirm, but it is well known at that very creek, from the explanation of the Testament, comparatively with the tides meeting to this day, he was set on shore.

The Maltese have erected an elegant church to the memory of St. Paul, with lively paintings all round of his shipwreck, shaking the snake off, barbarians coming with astonishment, etc. etc. There is a cave near this church where they say St. Paul lived con-cealed from the fury of the barbarians and likewise catacombs, which is a subterraneous passage that did extend six miles to the capital town. This was appro-priated at first to bury the dead, which gave an immense trouble to cut out the different apartments of all sizes to correspond with the bodies. In the war with the Christians and barbarians, the former lived concealed here, which answered the purpose very well after they laid in a sufficient quantity of provi-sions. The graves served them to sleep in and the intermediate spaces to eat and drink.

I had the pleasure of remaining during carnival

time, the different diversions being very entertaining. Masquerading was performed in the greatest perfection every night and, during the day, every person in the streets was masqued. The first interview I had, I was put in a state of consternation to behold such a group of transmogrified figures: men dressed like women and vice versa, some of the masques resembling pigs' heads and every uncouth shape that could be invented by the heads of men. Masquerading is a very convenient and suitable way for intrigue with the ladies, or, in other words, criminal connection and is carried on in the highest perfection, not only at Malta but in every other country, even in London.

We expected daily orders to proceed to England, and at last they came, but on the contrary was to survey a dangerous reef of rocks near Tunis, a kingdom of Africa, where several supposed rocks lay, as a number of ships were lost in that direction but not a soul saved to give an account.

As we had a number of dangers to encounter in searching for these unknown rocks, a man-of-war cutter was sent with us, that in case we should strike would be ready to take us in. We went to the island of Sicily to procure pilots, where we passed a few months. I landed first at that ancient place called Syracuse. St. Paul on his way as prisoner to Rome stayed here three days. It was once a very fine city but almost ruined by an earthquake in 1673.[64]

Gentlemen upon their travels explore this place with accuracy and find a number of antiques which give great satisfaction to the antiquarians. It was here that the famous mathematician Archimedes was put to death.[65]

Our antiquarian guide took us first to show Dionysius' cave, who was a terrible tyrant and had this built on purpose to exercise his savage brutality. This is the most curiously constructed cave in the world. Dionysius had a small opening at the top where he would, unseen, clap his ear to it, as this went all along the top of the cave which in shape resembles the human ear. Not a prisoner could whisper without his knowledge: when they would be lamenting their hard fate and rendering each other consolation and expatiating upon the tyranny of their confiner in the lowest accents, yet their cruel king would hear them and torture them accordingly. I have tore a piece of paper in the cave and it made a report like a gun, likewise fired a pistol which resembled thunder.

We went next to view the Catacombs and Mount Hebba, where the celebrated poet Virgil wrote part of his *Georgics* upon the bees and honey with which this mountain to this day abounds. Little did I suppose when learning this part at school that ever I would have the pleasure of seeing it, but this site recompensed me for all my puzzling lessons. The fountain of Arethusa is worthy of notice from the various romantic accounts in fabulous history, likewise the remains of a temple 3000 years old dedicated to Jupiter Olympus.

Syracuse is a small place but contains a great number of nobility who were extremely polite to us, paid every attention in their power to make us happy. Our first invitation was from the Baron de Busko to attend a *conversatione* (in Italian), which is an assembly of gentlemen and ladies, where they converse, play cards etc. etc. As none but the first select parties are permitted, makes it pleasant to pass a winter's night and you have an opportunity to be introduced and become acquainted.

Upon my entrance into the Baron's, I was much confounded on being interrogated as to what languages I could speak, particularly as the questions proceeded from the lips of a charming young lady, the Baron's sister. After asking me could I speak Italian, French, Spanish etc. etc. and my answering in the negative, she said to her companions that I was like a Turk, could speak no other language properly than my own native. I never felt so chagrined in all my life and cursed my hard fate that I had not been taught the French language. Indeed, in that country a gentleman's education is not considered complete except they can speak more living languages than their own. This is a very necessary accomplishment to young men that go abroad. What an unpleasant thing to be in a company where you cannot understand or be understood. This excited me to make profound application to improve in the Italian language, and as I frequently visited that house at the different routs and balls etc. etc., I became greatly enamoured with this young lady. From her prattling, the pains and pleasure she took in instructing me and from what I understood before of this language, I was soon capable of conversing well with her. All Italians are very attentive and in place of laughing if you make a mistake, they will rectify and anticipate your expressions.

The several months that I was backwards and forwards, I laid close siege to my *inamorato* and brought it with her and her parents' consent to the point of nuptial bonds, but could not take place from the laws of the country between a Protestant and a Roman Catholic without the consent of the Pope of Rome. The letter was forwarded accordingly and in the interval I went seven miles into the country with the British consul to visit his sick daughter. I was so pleased with his beautiful country house, the adjacent country so rural and fertile in the various luxuriant fruits – grapes, figs, olives, dates, almonds, apricots, pomegranates, etc. etc. (what a contrast between this and the Irish haw, black sloe and apples etc. etc!) – hospitable entertainment, riding excursions about the country, sweet Italian music, fair female society and everyone endeavouring to out vie the other to be the most attentive to the English Doctor, excited me to remain three weeks, having liberty to remain that time as no person on board was sick. This in some degree compensated for my toils and fatigues in Egypt and other places.

I went to visit a number of families (nobility). The Baron de Targo, for once prescribing to his sick daughter, sent me a very polite letter with two casks of superior old wine and two tremendous cheeses. Money, of course, I would not accept as it would degrade and vilify the character of the Navy Surgeon.

All the houses near the sea are built like castles in order to defend them from their enemies, the Tunisians and Tripolitans, who often land in the night and carry away whole families and make them slaves for life. I shall explain this more fully when at Tunis. I have often thought on the blessings of old England; you can go to bed without any terror which those people are continually involved in. No wonder liberty is sweet!

I got into a very extensive practice; the Governor of Syracuse offered me a house free if I would return and set up business. The long wished for letter had not yet arrived from Rome, which increased my fair intended's and my impatience. To pass the time more agreeably, I went a second time into the country with a gentleman to see the ancient papyrus. In the early ages they made use of stones, wax, ivory, etc. etc. The Egyptian paper mentioned by Latin authors was made of the rush papyrus. I gave a piece of this ancient papyrus to my brother Rev. Jn° Lowry, Ireland (which was considered a great favour by the donor to me, with his name on it). It is well worthy of inspection by the antiquarian. I became intimately acquainted with this gentleman and made him my companion whilst I remained at Syracuse. On my departure he gave me a letter of recommendation to his wife at Palermo requesting her to use me as she would himself.

The long looked for letter from the Pope[66] at last arrived, informing the Baron that I must appear in Rome before I could procure the dispensing order. This I could not do at present as His Majesty's service would not admit it. Any person may easy guess at my disappointment. I was quite irritated and said that the Pope was nothing but a hypocrite and this treatment was only ceremonial priestcraft. Upon the whole it happened very fortunately that I did not succeed: in the first place a sailor has no business with a wife; in the second, she had little money, although her brother lived in the most splendid and superb style; he kept three coaches. It is a very unfair and hard case that after the death of the father the whole property should fall to the lot of the eldest son;

the juniors' and females' fortunes are left to his option and discretion. Money is scarce in this island and a number has only empty titles.

We set sail with a favourable gale to that beautiful city Palermo, the capital of Sicily, called by the Latin poets Conca D'Oro, Auria Valli, Hortus Sicilae. I proceeded to deliver my letter of introduction (which I procured at Syracuse) to Mrs. A. and on my entrance into a very elegant house, the very lady, who expected me, met me at the door and presented to me my own card, which I had left when visiting her husband, and in return I gave her the letter. After the usual salutations and hearty welcomes to her abode, she introduced me to her mother, a baroness, and would be happy if I would drink tea with her that evening and take a ride in her coach on the Marina (a place of resort and pleasure near the seaside).[67] I declined, having a prior appointment. Before we parted, she made me declare that I would make her house my home, use her coach whenever inclined and dine with her the next day. I congratulated myself on my good quarters and would take care not to be deprived of the honour of her kind offer.

There was a great contrast between my present circumstances and the time I was here as assistant surgeon. I was now possessed of plenty of money, well acquainted, therefore I had no restraint in fulfilling my wishes and entering into the first genteel society.

In all my leisure hours I resorted to Mrs. A., where I became similar to one of the family. No wonder: there were great attractions, a fine lady to discourse with, two liveried servants to drive us in the coach every evening on the Marina and all attention showed me that was the least conducive to my happiness.

This was quite a new change. To ride in this style, grant attendance, lighted in and out of the carriage at night by two large flambeaux, exhilarated my spirits to the highest degree – vanity, vanity, the root of all evil. My pleasure was too great to reflect upon any past situation. I always make it a rule to be comfortable whilst in my power.

I communicated my intention to Mrs. A. of exploring this beautiful city. She immediately consented to accompany me in all my excursions and in the course of one week would pledge her honour that I should be satisfied in all my curiosity.

We first drove in the coach to that handsome square called Ottanglo which is adorned with uniform buildings. From this square I had a view of all the fine streets and the four great gates of the city; Porta Nuova and Porta Felice, very much admired for the elegance of their architecture. After scrutinising these and other parts with accuracy, she entertained me the next day by showing me the chapels, which are very numerous and extremely rich. The cathedral is a large ancient gothic structure, supported by eighty columns of oriental granite, which is separated into a number of chapels. That of St. Rosalia, which saint is considered the patroness of Palermo, is extremely grand. The relics of this saint are preserved in a large silver box wrought and enriched with precious stones. They pretend to work many miracles with them and that they will never be attacked with the plague as long as they are in possession. They relate that prior to her death she walked round the city and saved it from that pestilential disorder. However, her relics are considered one of the greatest treasures of the city. Every town in Sicily has its tutelar saint, richly ornamented with gold, silver and every precious stone. Palermo is crowded with them, placed in the squares upon pedestals.

The following day we went to a most celebrated convent of Capuchins, about a mile from Palermo, in which there is a vault made for the reception of the dead. It has four wide passages about forty-four feet in length along the sides of which are niches to support the bodies upright, who are covered with coarse garments, with their heads, arms and feet bare.

They prepare them for this situation by broiling them six or seven months upon a gridiron over a slow fire until the fat is consumed. The skin continues entire and the countenance in some degree preserved.

On the floor are handsome trunks which contain the bodies of the nobility or other people of distinction. Both young and old often go and have niches fixed for their height to be in readiness.

I was greatly astonished at the different spectacles, the gloomy, dismal looking place. You could not turn round but what there were apparently ten or twelve dead bodies staring you in the face. This drove me for a little into a melancholy reverie upon our transitory life, poor mortal frame, etc. etc. When after my recovery, I heard the deep fetched sighs of my female companion, who had by this time popped into a corner to view her relatives. Here, says she, weeping, is my poor Grandpapa and Mama and my father and two sisters. Finding the longer she tarried, the more restless she became, I hurried her out to prevent any more unpleasant reflections. I continued very sad all that day.

I think this to be a good institution, as beholding the bodies of their relations may impress their memory with futurity and incline them to be more religious. Why should I talk of religion here? I ought to say cunning priestcraft and the custom of the Pharisees, all external ostentation, but little pure internal gospel.

This place as well as others in Sicily abound with monks, friars and mendicants. The latter have an appropriated convent and live entirely by begging.

Their garments are extremely coarse, which they wear without any shirt; likewise sandals, a thick sole tied with thongs round the foot.

After passing a month with a great degree of pleasantry, we received orders to convey the King of Naples to take possession of his kingdom, the rebellion being quelled and peace restored over all the world. This intelligence was by no means agreeable to me, as I might never have the felicity of seeing Palermo again. Sea officers are very uncomfortably situated in this point; when they have formed a pleasing set of acquaintance, they are obliged to part and probably never see them again.

Prior to the departure of the King, the captain of the *Medusa* frigate gave a grand ball on board his ship. A great number of the nobility of Palermo attended who were not a little surprised at the grand display and superb style of the entertainment. We danced to one o'clock, when above 200 couples sat down to supper, which cost the captain £500.[68] Afterwards the ladies favoured us with a few Italian songs accompanied by music. We passed the night with the greatest mirth and gaiety.

In four days we arrived in Naples, where every preparation was made as an emblem of their loyalty and hearty welcome of their king who, as I related before, was obliged to leave his country to save his life. The fireworks, illuminations, temporary amphitheatres, temporary temples erected after the manner of the ancients, far surpasses in elegance and taste any account that I can communicate. It cost upwards of £100,000 Sterling. Therefore it is easy to form an idea of its majestic splendour.

We brought over the Prince of Butero, his daughter, concubine and retinue in the *Weazle*; his wife, the Princess, went in the *Medusa* frigate. This excited my curiosity to investigate into the cause of such a singular custom. Mr. Roach, a wine merchant who had lived twelve years in the place, was likewise a passenger. He gave me a full account of the whole and the manners and customs of the Italian ladies, which I was greatly ignorant of before. The Prince, says he, although a married man, keeps several concubines, one of which you see, and the Princess, his wife, has her favourite *Cicisbeo* (a gallant) that cohabits with her.[69] It is very customary for every married man to have some favourite, either single or wedded, and his wife, her gallant.

The ladies in Italy and Sicily are by no means admired for their chastity, of which they possess a very small share, are very lascivious and amorous, often afflicted with *Furor Uterinae*.[70] The warm climate and every luxury of life excites their passions to venery. There is more excuse for them than females in cold climates. I will say this much for the Italian and French that they are more agreeable, lively, affable and full of vivacity than our English ladies.

The Princess at this time was afflicted with the venereal disease, which she contracted in some of her amours. I doubted the assertion at first, but it was actually the case, being informed by a surgeon that attended her who found the disease so far advanced that no medicine was of any utility. She died at Rome six months after she was landed at Naples. As we have a certain specific for this malady, I impeach her death to the ignorance of the surgeon or to her non-timely application.

This calls to remembrance a true story related to me by a captain of a man of war whilst he was in the company of Lady Hamilton and two princesses, the King of Naples' daughters. The former asked him could he speak Italian. He entered in the negative (although he could) in order to discover the secret which he had a distant hint from the first of their conversation. One of the latter, on hearing he did not understand, communicated to her companion how unfortunate she had been to contract the venereal complaint in the first amour with a young gentleman. The other gave her every consolation and sincerely wished that she would not be so unlucky in her next.

Hearing a number of these anecdotes about the fair females (I have given this as a specimen) and the unconcern of breaking the conjugal vow, I related the circumstance of my female companion at Palermo. I never saw a man to be more astonished in my life that I had not succeeded. Depend upon it, continued he, she will laugh at you for your simplicity and ignorance of the world and her esteem and attention would be greatly diminished. I began now to reflect upon the fine opportunities I let pass, but if ever I should see Palermo again I would atone for my past conduct. My former obstruction was breaking that Commandment, adultery, but rather than get in disgrace with the fair sex, I would change my idea and adhere to the old proverb, 'when we are in Rome do as Rome does'.

If I passed a pleasant time at Palermo, I now enjoyed myself as much at this beautiful city, Naples, where I was before when in the capacity of surgeon's mate but saw none of the curiosities for the want of money. The rejoicings for the return of the king lasted a fortnight. I shall never see anything again similar to its splendour. When finished I proceeded to see the various antiquities.

The *Weazle* stopped here two months. I took lodgings on shore and attended physical lectures and improved greatly in my profession. I employed my leisure hours in reviewing the different curiosities. I was highly delighted with the famous Mount Vesuvius. At times streams of lava issue from the volcano, likewise melted metal, sulphur, minerals run down the mountain like a torrent, which is three miles from the bottom to the summit. When I got near the top, the mountain was belching out ashes, fire and smoke. I heard a dreadful noise; my memory was impressed with the terror that if an eruption would take place, it would be inevitable destruction to me. Whole villages near this mountain with their inhabitants have been buried with the melted lava which has the resemblance of melted lead.

Not far off from this is the village of Portici, where I saw a great collection of antiquities, mostly dug out of the ruins of the ancient city Herculaneum, which was completely overwhelmed by the above matters in the reign of the Emperor Titus Anno. Dom. 79. Herculaneum has been only found out by digging (accidentally) and that but lately. It is well worthy of the stranger's attention to go through the subter-ranean passages where you will see part of the ruined houses. One in particular attracted my attention where the sign of a house of pleasure was painted over the door. I have seen signs of all description explaining what was to be sold but the sign of a penis above the door explaining the sale of prostitutes was entirely beyond my comprehension, and how the people in those days were so debauched and vitiated as to allow this astonished me and created a disgust.

On the road leading from the suburbs of Chiaiae to the Grotto del Pausilipo are the remains of the tomb of our famous poet Virgil. The keeper of this mausoleum makes a good sum of money per annum by shewing it to the curious and distributing the laurels which grow on it. The above grotto is cut through a mountain and is nearly three quarters of a mile long and at the entrance an immense height. I passed through this to see the Lake Agano and the sudatories[71] of St. German where water (which is sulphurous) is continually hot and very serviceable in some diseases. On the left side of the road leading thither are the best vines in the world: the very place where Virgil wrote that part of his *Georgics* about them.

In a rock near the bank of the lake is the Grotto del Cano (or dog's cave), so called because a man takes a dog for experiment and holds the animal above the cave. Foul air arises and suffocates him. This air will soon deprive any animal of life. This said air is called by chemists, according to the new nomenclature, Nitrogen gas, and also azotic gas – vulgo called atmospheric mephitis, this forms more than two thirds of the atmosphere we breathe in, but alone, which this cave abounds with, destroys animal life and combustion.[72]

The last few days of excursions I had at Naples were likely to be attended with serious consequences. My companion and I drove about as usual in a curricle through the streets. He was very frolicsome and jocose. Nothing could give him better diversion than to drive near the cobblers' stalls and upset them who sit outside of doors and work, particularly in the morning before sunrise; and it is no small curiosity to see these cobblers occupying a whole street. We upset two, which passed very well as we soon galloped from them. In our great haste a shaft of our curricle hauled a man down and the wheels ran right over him. We stopped and a great mob assembled round us exclaiming against the rash accident. We had great difficulty to appease them. After examining I found him not materially injured and by giving him £6 compromised the affair. We rode away with great exultation that he was not killed.

There is not a city in the world that produces the necessities and luxuries of life in greater profusion, yet there are a number of poor who are obliged to spend the night in the streets as well as the day. There are an immense number of monks, fiddlers, pipers, lazzaronies and pimps. A stranger cannot walk twenty yards without being attacked by pimps crying in Italian, '*Margurita, Seniore, bella juvena, picanina,*' which means 'Will you have a prostitute? She is handsome, young and little.' If you frown at the word *picanina* (little) they will immediately say, '*Oh Seniore, multo grosso*', 'she is large'. The connoisseur of this article may have them at all sizes and ages from twelve to thirty years old. The pimps are employed by those lewd women to procure them customers and gain their livelihood in this way.

Often I have gone in company with other gentlemen to see these fair damsels. This city contains an amazing number who live, at least some of them, in an elegant style, liveried servants to attend them. One house in particular shined in splendour. A liveried servant came to the door with a lighted torch in his hand, his dress trimmed with gold and silver tinsel (which, by the way, is very cheap), conducted us up into a very spacious and rich apartment where three beautiful females received us with the greatest cordiality, painted like Jezebel, dressed with such fine muslins that you might see their shapes to the greatest nicety, their breasts exposed in the most wanton manner, heads decorated and wreathed with pearls and artificial flowers, hair hanging down their bosoms in beautiful ringlets, lascivious attitudes, their breath as fragrant as the spices of Arabia. Alas! what human depravity and art excited us to stop and treat them with a few bottles of wine. They give us some Italian sweet airs upon the harpsichord and guitar which made us pass the winter's evening very jovial. I have often been sorry to behold so many charming females prostitute themselves to gain their livelihood.

Our captain being very desirous to behold the fireworks of Palermo, communicated his intention of returning to pass another month at that city, which gave me great pleasure that I should be gratified with another sight of Mrs. A. and have an opportunity of retrieving my lost esteem.

7. Sicilian Survey, 1802–3

WE ANCHORED AT THE mole at Palermo but that evening I could not get on shore from a misunderstanding between our captain and 1st. lieutenant. However, the next day she sent her coach for me. On our first salutation she seemed quite distant and displeased that I should remain so long without paying her a visit. I satisfied her of my inability and of the tormenting anxiety I was troubled with since my arrival upon her account, but as I now had been blessed with the sight of her lovely face she could not deny me the favour of a salutation of her lips which, being accepted, we became as mutual friends as ever. I considered this a very necessary step towards the accomplishment of my wishes, which I was convinced would be very easy provided I had impudence – but why should I say impudence when it is customary for every married woman to have her *Cicisbeo* as mentioned before. I only required confidence; she gave me plenty of opportunities.

That same evening the fireworks commenced and she proposed going to a friend's house to meet a party of ladies and then we should all proceed together. She dressed in very great style – the Parisian fashions had but lately arrived. Including her necklaces, it could not have cost less than £400. I was introduced to a number of ladies and gentlemen who were all prepared for the entertainment. To my infinite sorrow, all the females went into one coach and the gentlemen into another.

There were about 500,000 spectators at this extraordinary phenomenon which takes place once a year and costs upward of £20,000. It is prepared by the sea side and is set afire at dark. To my wonderful consternation, a great part of the sea close to the Marina seemed in a blaze, the fire came roaring out of the water like peals of thunder when the great works on the Marina began. I now had a view of most of the inhabitants of the city, who were seated in appropriated places above each another. I was convinced that the remarks of different authors were true, that this island produced the most charming women in the world.

These fire works are of a most singular and curious construction, made by powder *stratum super stratum*, folded and placed upon wheels. At times it will appear similar to sea and land battles; at others, serpents and different animals which causes the igneous scene to be delightful and astonishing.

I accompanied my fair female home, where she treated me with a few ice creams, which are very pleasant and palatable in these warm climates. They have plenty of snow all summer, which is brought from Mount Etna and preserved in vaults from dissolving.

One evening I obtained the conquest. I pressed my lips to her cheeks and by some unavoidable stumble, we both fell down. As Sterne says,

> yes and then – ye whose cold clay lips and lukewarm hearts can argue down or mask your passions, tell me, what trespass is it that man should have them? or how his spirit stands answerable to the Father of Spirits but for his conduct under them? If nature has so wove her web of kindness that some threads of love and desire are entangled within the piece – must the whole web be rent in drawing them out? Whip me such stoics, great Governor of nature! said I to myself. Wherever thy providence shall place me for the trials of my virtue, whatever is my danger, whatever it is my situation – let me feel the movements that rise out of it and which belong to me as a man – and if I govern them as a good one, I will trust the issues to thy justice, for thou hast made us and not we ourselves.[73]

We left this place and went round Sicily, calling at every seaport town. I had an opportunity of seeing a great number of curiosities at Gargenta,[74] which stands about six miles from the sea, and when we landed the English consul sent us two light horse to protect us from the numerous banditti who often pillage the antiquarian traveller. The temples of Apollo, Hercules, and Giants are very worthy of remark for their structure and antiquity. The latter is in complete ruins. Men were employed to raise the stones which were of an immense weight. The dimensions of one in particular I lost with my other documents when I was shipwrecked. They likewise dig up vases and other household furniture of a most curious shape and construction. These together with the temples are of 1880 years standing. I suppose the utensils were buried by an earthquake. Here I saw the tomb of our great father of physic Aesculapius. His sons Machaon and Podilarius are the supporters on the seal of the Royal College of Surgeons, London.

There is a whispering church in Gargenta, so called because if you stand in one end of it and speak as low as possible, an other person at the other end, although a great distance, will understand and answer you by the same low accents. This is like the whispering gallery in St. Pauls Church, London.

We next steered our course to that ancient city Catania, which stands near Mount Etna. It has been often destroyed by earthquakes, and in the last 18,000 people were buried in the ruins. We did not tarry long here as it was our intention to explore the above famous burning mount, which is continually emitting flames of fire, lava etc. etc. We found it extremely hot as we commenced our journey at the bottom, which in some places emits sulphurous vapours. Having arrived about the middle after a tedious circumambulate that we were obliged to make on account of its steepness, where we began to feel colder and to increase gradually as we approached the region of snow. We regaled on a little meat and drink in a small hut that a man keeps and gains his livelihood by supplying travellers with flannels, which we dressed in previous to our proceeding amongst the snow. Only for this alteration we could not bear the sudden extreme from heat to cold. At times we were up to our knees in snow; at others in danger of being overwhelmed in it. I repented my undertaking, yet as my companions were so anxious, I bore it with patience. At last we gained our point by going as near the volcano as not to receive any injury from the lava etc. What a singular phenomenon! At the bottom excessive heat; above the middle and towards the summit, snow; from the volcano at the summit, flames of fire and smoke issuing out with great conflagration.

We left Catania and set sail for Messina. When passing along the coast of Calabria, I was very much surprised at its appearance, the irregularity of the country. This together with Messina suffered more from the tremendous earthquakes than any other part of the world.

The following account taken from history may be interesting.

> Great part of Calabria and Sicily was destroyed in the beginning of 1783 by an earthquake, than which, there are few more dreadful upon record. It destroyed many cities and villages, farms out of number and above 4000 inhabitants, mountains were levelled and valleys were formed in an instant. New rivers was given to flow and old streams was sunk in the earth and destroyed. Plantations were removed from their situation and hills carried to places far distant. At Casel Nuova the Prince of Gerace and upwards of 4000 of the inhabitants lost their lives; at Ragnara 3107; at Radicina and Palma 6000; at Terra Nuova 1400.

We proceeded through the Faro di Messina where the tide runs so very rapid that it was called by the ancients Charybdis (whirlpool). Either Horace or Virgil mentions it, which I believe runs nearly thus:

> If you from Charybdis shun,
> You will upon Scylla run[75]

or this: 'The rocks of Scylla on his eastern side, while in the west, with hideous yawns disclosed, his onward path Charybdis gulf opposed.' In those days seamanship was not well understood, which made this place exceedingly dangerous. When the above lines was wrote, Scylla, which was then a ridge of rocks, was entirely destroyed by the above earthquake in 1783. A wave which had swept the country for three miles carried off on its return 2473 of the inhabitants at Scylla with the prince at their head.

I often imagined when perusing the Latin authors that the greatest part was mere fiction, but I am now convinced to the contrary that they had a good foundation for all their assertions (*experentia docet*).[76] At Messina the ruined houses still stand ever since the dreadful earthquake.

The reason that these countries are so subject to earthquakes is from the burning of Mount Vesuvius, Etna and Stromboli, which latter is one of the Lipari Islands and although the least burns the best, which I have often experienced. It has a most awful appearance in the night from its belching out huge stones in the air that are plainly perceived at a great distance from it, continually emitting fire and flames and causes great illumination. It has almost rendered the island uninhabitable. Sir William Hamilton has given an excellent description of these mountains which are the cause of the earthquakes. The earth underneath is consumed which renders a hollow and the upper will fall in and cause a tremendous concussion.

I need not discuss much upon this town as it is like all others in Sicily in point of customs and manners. I passed here many a pleasant day as I have been there thirty different times. The last time before my departure, my body was nearly being left amongst the Sicilian clay.

One evening I walked home with a young beautiful damsel, where I tarried so long, she advised me to stop all night, my frame being made of such materials that it never could resist female persuasion. At a very late hour in the night, a man came to our room door, made a tremendous noise, '*Aperto la porta, subito, subito*' (open the door immediately) or he would break it all to atoms. Every knock was harder and harder. She trembled to such a degree that the bed shaked under her. She cried for the assistance of a number of saints, St. Lucia, St. Rosalia, etc. etc. but finding no relief, changed her yells to '*Maria Virginia veni ca, veni ca*' (come here, come here), requested me to take care otherwise he would stab me. This I was well aware of, knowing that she was his kept mistress. From the tenor of her prayers, his threats, although in a little danger, I could not avoid smiling.

At last he succeeded in breaking open the door. I was now in a curious predicament, but little afraid, from having a charged pistol in each hand. One indeed is sufficient to intimidate twenty Italians, where a sword would have no effect, as they are very dexterous in parrying off with their cloaks and then thrusting their long daggers or stiletto into you. I presented my pistols and conjured him not to proceed a step further, otherwise he would be instantaneously a dead man. His countenance became pale, his features shrunk (which I distinguished from a glimmering light that proceeded from an oil lamp which is generally kept burning all night in those houses), begged for the love of Maria Virginia to spare his life and he would retire directly. This I condescended to, provided he would adhere to the following stipulations: 1st, let me remain quietly in the habitation tonight, 2^{ly}, not to come or send any person to molest me.

I could not put much confidence in this treaty; my sleep was disturbed the remainder of the night. On hearing the least noise, I construed it into some person coming with a naked dagger to stab me. What a blessing, says I to myself, that pistols were contrived and that I would not give them at present for a thousand pounds. At break of day I sallied forth without presenting any emoluments to my fair damsel, informing her at the same time, in place of a night's good repose, it happened to be one of pain. I met with a little obstruction at the outer door from the mother who bellowed lustily '*Sensa pagare*' (without payment). A great number of mothers prostitute their daughters to gain their livelihood. From my maltreatment, I was callous to all solicitations and informed them that the Devil would have them all without deep penitent reformation.

I took particular care to walk in the middle of the streets, as it was only peep of day, imagining one of these lurking banditti might assassinate me from a corner. I spied a light in a coffee house, where I entered and refreshed myself with a cup. My mind was more refreshed when I considered my liberation and fortunate escape.

I had not remained here three hours until I received the intelligence of an English officer lying dead in a small garden in the suburbs. I went thither in order to satisfy myself whether it was any of my acquaintance. Alas! whom did I behold, but Mr. Taylor, our captain's clerk. The evening preceding this disaster we had been in company with each other. He was intoxicated. I learned that shortly after I left him, he went out and fell in with some murderer who took him to this garden, stripped him of his hat, coat and boots (probably about the time I was in the above dilemma), barbarously cut him across the scalp three times and introduced their stiletto into his heart. I felt the emotions of grief and rage, the former for the victim and the latter against the inhuman murderer. Alas! a fine young man cut off in the flower of his youth was sufficient to excite the greatest sorrow.

Being time for our captain to proceed on his survey, we went to Trapani or Trapano, a town of Val di Mazara[77] of this island, where we procured pilots and set out on our grand and important object to a place called by the fishermen Squirquies, where we anchored on a bank out of sight of land and sounded these shoals, but did not succeed. We were highly entertained in fishing, as multitudes were in this part. We caught more than the whole ship's company could eat. We returned after a fortnight to Trapani and, although a small place, I may well say that the three weeks we remained was a complete jubilee.

We returned to finish our survey and on our passage we got aground on a sandbank, where our ship struck very hard. We were in the most eminent danger for twenty-four hours, and only for the timely assistance of seven fishing boats we should never have got off, and consequently been all lost. We were obliged to throw all our provisions overboard to lighten the ship.

We put back to Trapani and got more and then sailed for Squirquies. Nothing could be more fortunate than when we arrived and, having all our sail set, we were near striking upon a rock that was only one foot above the surface. This proved to be the said shoal we were searching for and where many a ship with all the souls on board perished, which is clearly proved from us discovering guns, parts of ships near this ridge of rocks. We named it Lord Keith's Shoal and all the Christian part of the world now knows the bearance and distance that will prevent shipwrecks here in futurity. What could be more dangerous than a shoal of this nature, out of sight of land and, when the sea is a little rough, out of sight of the mariner. If a ship with all sail set strikes against it, she will go to the bottom in one moment, no one will be left to relate the event. We returned again to Trapani and then went to other different parts of Sicily where we remained a few days but met with nothing worthy of mentioning.

We received orders to go to Malta and from thence to that uninhabited island Lampadosa[78] which the French offered us, during the treaty, for Malta. We remained here for six weeks per order of our government until the captain had finished surveying it and whether he could procure fresh water and that the stones would answer to make lime, in which he succeeded. Although the French made several trials, they could never find any water. A great number of people are buried here who died with the plague that were sent to this island to perform quarantine. We occupied all our leisure hours in shooting birds of all descriptions, rabbits, hares. No person need ever starve here whilst he has a gun, powder and shot.

We returned to Malta, where our captain received further orders to reconnoitre the French and Spanish ports to ascertain whether they were making any active preparations for a war in their arsenals. Although peace, we had a jealous eye towards each other.

We proceeded first to that beautiful city Marseilles in France, where I spent my time very agreeably among the French gentlemen and ladies for one month. Although we have been and will probably be eternal enemies, every degree of attention is extended to each other with mutual consent when we meet in private parties. This is requisite for the good of society.

We next steered our course to Toulon, where I fell in with a few acquaintances that I had formed when prisoner there. I remained on shore for six weeks, was quite pleased with the various amusements, particularly in the company of the sprightly French ladies, who are greatly admired for their vivacity and pleasantry but not in the least for their chastity in keeping the nuptial vow. They are much like in this point to the Italians.

The lower class of people, even the very peasants, are extremely polite. Politeness is the great characteristic of this nation and they are deserving of that name. As we are nothing but birds of passage in the Navy, where we can make the most free at first sight, of course we esteem it the best.

It is necessary for every young man that goes abroad, who wishes to be acquainted with the manners and customs of the people, to enter into their society and amusements, for which he must spare no expenses, otherwise he will leave the city or place as ignorant as when he went in.

I attended the masquerades, which are so famous for intrigues. It cost me half a guinea a night for my dress. I went in the character of a clown. Not being capable to speak the French, this answered me best. I met with three brother clowns, but I certainly excelled them, having a tremendous mouth on my mask. Staring at everything I saw with astonishment, the more I could resemble a plebeian or a country-man that never had seen a city, the better I performed my character.

When a French gentlemen or lady, whether single or married, wishes to intrigue, masquerading is famous for that design. Previous to their going, inform each other of their dress, and if they please, which is often practised, the gentlemen may mask and dress similar to a lady and the lady like the gentlemen so that from appearance you will be mistaken in the sex. If the stranger to those sports is not cautious and has a distant hint of this scheme, he may take a partner to a dance with him whom he has every reason to suppose is a female but on the termination of the country dance, to his utter astonishment, proves to be a male, which causes a general laugh by him unmasking.

Those that come with the intention of intriguing may succeed without ever being discovered by the husband or any person else. After dancing they retire to a private room (which is kept convenient for that purpose) and indulge in Venus, then return to the company. Those again that do not come with the intention of carrying on any bad design, will dance all night with their most intimate friends and acquaintances without knowing each other and, in order to make the discovery and cause greater diversion, will sit down to supper unmasked. They will be very much surprised. Who would have the least idea! that it was my friend dressed like a Merry-Andrew, another in the character of a clown, a third of a sailor, a fourth of a mountebank, a fifth as a cart driver, a sixth Sylvanus, seventh a face like a pig who answers by grunts, eighth a Turk, ninth an ancient Roman warrior, tenth a sweep, milk maids and goddesses. Indeed, numerous are the different characters and the higher the more expensive. If you will appear like the Grand Signior,[79] your dress must be ornamented with gold and silver and your turban decorated with precious stones, at least mock stones.

I dined every day at what the French call *table d'hote* (ordinary) with a number of Dutch, Portuguese, Spanish and French officers; very cheap provided I had paid daily, but I kept a running score and the innkeeper charged (or rather cheated) me the exorbitant sum of £50 for all expenses. But old birds are not to be caught with chaff. I brought him before a Justice of the Peace and had it diminished, after a great deal of trouble, to one half. Every nation endeavours to impose upon the English because they are more liberal than any other, particularly sailors. I made several excursions into the country villages with gentlemen on their travels, who, I am sorry to say, on the commencement of hostilities were detained in France.[80]

We left this and went to Barcelona in Spain and from thence to Alicant, where I was highly entertained by a number of Irish merchants and, as an English man of war had seldom been at that place, they thought that they never could pay too great attention to us. They gave us, the month we remained, most superb dinners, balls, routs, etc. etc. which made the time exceeding short. I admired the Spanish ladies for their fine black eyes, but they are not possessed of that vivacity which is so natural to the French and Italians. Jealousy, which this nation was so much addicted to they would even run a man through upon the least suspicion, seems to be greatly diminished and that amorous vice which is so prevalent in other countries is now less or more sanctioned, particularly by the Spanish Dons.

We proceeded to Cartagena, a famous seaport town of Murcia in Spain. The foundation was laid

225 years before Christ when it received the appellation of Carthago Nova, named after the ancient Carthage. The King of Spain had but lately passed through this town and for his amusement they erected amphitheatres, commenced their great bull fights, operas and plays that the short time we remained it was very entertaining.

Our next place was to that barbarous place Algiers in Africa. As we did not stop long, I had little opportunity of remarking. They speak a great deal of that language called *Lingua Franca*, which consists of Latin, French, Italian and Spanish. At last we obtained the length of Gibraltar. As I had letters of recommendation from Alicant to several gentlemen and ladies at this barren rock, I was as usual highly entertained whilst our ship was refitting.

Afterwards we left this and arrived at Malta after a passage of seven weeks. We were obliged to proceed once more to Lampadosa and upon our return from that to Malta. To our infinite satisfaction, Sir Richd Bickerton's squadron had sailed to Naples, and expected daily the account of another war commenced between Great Britain and France, where we joined him in the course of two days. In June 1803 our orders arrived to capture and destroy all French ships.

8. To War Again, June 1803

THE GALLANT ADMIRAL ALLOWED us to cruise a month off the island of Sardinia to intercept the Levant trade and, only for contrary winds which prevented the ships coming from the Levant, we should have all made an immense fortune. As it happened, we took two rich ships the very day our cruise expired and sent our prizes to the island of Malta, and we joined Lord Nelson off Toulon. We fell in with another ship, which we captured after a long chase and great difficulty under the French batteries in sight of Lord Nelson's fleet.

At this time we were in quarantine, therefore none of the other ships would receive our prisoners as it would put them in the same situation. They exceeded in number our men, which obliged us to go armed night and day to be prepared in case of an insurrection, which they attempted on our passage to Malta, but instantaneously shooting a few of them soon quelled them. We landed them on the quarantine ground, or a place where, if any person has any communication with a nation subject to the plague, is obliged to remain forty days, allowing, should there be any lurking contagion, it will appear in that space of time.

Our next orders from Malta were to proceed to Tripoli in Africa with dispatches to the British consul. The inhabitants of this place have been for ages remarked for their piracies. They are complete barbarians. The consul, who first went over as physician to the Bey (or king), got this vacancy, which he still holds, having resigned his profession for the consulship as it was more lucrative (than the other): £1000 per annum.

As he was once a brother in profession, paid me particular attention. I lived with him a month, which gave me a famous opportunity to see the manners and customs of those people; seldom any European has that opportunity, as they carry on no traffic and live by the produce of their land and piracies. The curious and antiquarian traveller dare never resort in the interior for he would not return alive, particularly on the frontiers of Biledulgerid.[81] The natives are lewd, treacherous, thievish and barbarously savage. Robbery and murder are their chief delights.

The Bey's admiral, who was a Scotchman and to his disgrace turned to the Mahometan religion, previous to his obtaining this high situation was very fortunate in capturing Sardinian, Italian and Sicilian ships, and likewise landing his sailors in the night, stripping whole villages of men and women and children who were made slaves during their lives. He had fifteen wives and I often jeered and solicited him, over a bottle of wine, to show them to me. In answer he said that he would, with the greatest of pleasure, only it was against their religious laws and regulations.

I made several attempts at his house to spy them, but all in vain, until one evening whilst in the state of intoxication I persuaded him to let me see his black wife. A better made woman could not be produced, her features elegant, countenance expressive and charming, her colour a fine glossy jet black, deportment noble and, upon the whole, a most admirable woman. The variety for her to see me was as great as mine, for she had not seen a man, except her husband, this fifteen years and that time was her father.

The Bey had a very large seraglio (or a house of women of pleasure) which contained one hundred wives and as many concubines. No man is ever allowed to enter except the eunuchs and a doctor upon the same restrictions I entered. The former keep watch day and night: woe! be unto the first that is even seen looking, with or without a suspicious eye. His head would be instantly severed from his body upon the spot. There is no courts of justice in this country and lives are considered of no value.

When the Bey wishes to make one his bedfellow, he

acquaints the governess, who gets her washed and perfumed and leads her into the bedchamber. If a favourite, she may get in at the side of the bed, but on the contrary must creep in at the foot. In this way he takes his wives and concubines in rotation. Formerly he did not, but took those first that pleased him the most in dancing and singing; consequently this created a number of jealous disputes amongst the fair damsels.

The Bey sent for me to visit two of his wives. I hesitated at first, not wishing to trust myself with these barbarian eunuchs, as I probably might be induced to bestow a complacent smile which would be jealously construed and consequently the above punishment. After repeated solicitations, I consented and was conducted to the Bey's house. They perfumed me by sprinkling rose water over me according to the custom of the east, as I walked through a hall attended by a number of these stout sturdy Turks. When I arrived the length of the seraglio and expected to have seen my two patients, I was informed by an interpreter that I must prescribe without seeing them. I felt their pulses as they stood behind a curtain and gave them at random a little cooling medicine.

Upon my exit I was like Lot's wife, looked behind me and saw a number of female faces peeping. I immediately recollected my critical situation and walked on without any more hesitation. I received some very handsome presents to the amount of £20.

The Bey at this time was involved in war. The mountaineers killed his relation and to be revenged marched 30,000 of his soldiers to kill and destroy all they could find. I saw this formidable army march or, more properly struggle, out of Tripoli, previous to which he distributed handfuls of gold amongst them. What rendered it more formidable was the immense number of camels and dromedaries.

When I saw at a little distance 4000 of these huge beasts with soldiers on their backs who were dressed in large cloaks with hoods, I could not avoid supposing them to be many moving mountains. They likewise had a number of elephants. This is a tremendous animal, capable of drawing with ease as much as six or seven horses and can support four thousand pounds weight upon its back and one thousand upon its trunk. If pushed on it will go a hundred miles in a day, but fifty or sixty with facility.

Every morning the heads of these unfortunate victims were hung upon the gates at the entrance of the city for the inspection of the Bey. I often rode out a mile in the country with the European consuls. I never could pass the gates without seriously reflecting upon these dreadful spectacles; after eight o'clock it was almost impossible for us to endure the heat.

I saw that cruel punishment inflicted called

*Rough sketch of an elephant taken at Tripoli, a
republic in Africa*

bastinado, which is beating on the soles of the feet
with a stick until they are reduced to a mere mash.
They are hardly ever able to walk afterwards. This is
considered a worse punishment than even death,
which they would prefer before the other, but if the
crime is great it would be considered too noble for
them to lose their head.

These people are very ignorant, not the least kind
of literature or books amongst them except the Al
Koran. Some of them can write a little with a reed or

cane in place of quills. Before they assemble to their mosques, two or three walk round making a great noise by bellowing out, 'All you good believers of Mahomet assemble and worship.' A number of the men go almost naked; fools and silly people, not even one rag to cover any part. Those are considered of a superior race and are revered.

Sodomy is not considered a crime, yet not so much countenanced as at other places. I went three miles to see a man with two horns growing out of his head. By the by, it may not be amiss to remark that this was a disease of the skull and not what they supposed, a mixed propagation with brutes. I have been informed that in the interior they are nothing better than beasts and some of them had tails like sheep; how far authentic I will not presume to assert.

The consul of Denmark was a great naturalist, had a large collection of animals well arranged and a few of the tribe of the six classes of Linnaeus: mammalia, birds, amphibious animals, fishes, insects and worms.[82] He presented me with a crocodile, viper, scorpion and a tarantula, all preserved in spirits. The former was young. Some of the old ones are twenty-five feet in length and as thick as a man's body. A number are in the river Nile, but not as many as formerly. This is a formidable and dangerous animal. It will lie concealed amongst the reeds and rushes, at a little distance resemble the old trunk of a tree, at an

Rough sketch of a young crocodile presented to me in spirits by the plenipotentiary of Denmark

instant spring and seize a man or beast and devour them.

The bite of the tarantula is cured by musick, an instance of which I saw at Taranto in Naples.[83] The fiddle had not the desired effect but the violincello, fiddle and flute had.

I bought an ostrich for fifteen dollars. I was informed afterwards by Mr. Brooke, Professor of Zootomy in London, that he would have given me £90 for it had I brought it to England, in which I could not succeed – being so troublesome on board our ship, I was obliged to send it on shore. This bird

Rough sketch of an ostrich, the largest of all the feathered tribe

is the largest of all the feathered tribe and is eight feet
high from the top of its head to the ground, can digest
anything: the two days it was on board ate two quarts
of old nails and pieces of iron; seemed to be very
partial to iron – it would pick at the nails drove into
the deck. I have been told, they will eat anything
indiscriminately and never drink. I have been highly
entertained from the top of a small mountain looking

at hundreds of these going twice as swift as race horses along the scorching uninhabitable and sandy deserts which place they frequent. Every female in England is fond of that expensive article, ostrich feathers. And no wonder: it is a great ornament to the head-dress.

A number of Jews live at Tripoli; why should I say here? The predilection is very true: 'Thou shall be a wandering tribe and have no nation of your own.' I have seen and heard of them being in the most remote parts of the world. The Jewesses are in general handsome. The barbarian Jewesses dress in a most curious and singular style. We could always have free ingress and egress into their houses but never durst attempt to even look into the Turks' upon the peril of losing our lives.

We bid adieu to all the consuls, except the French, who parted with us with some degree of reluctance. Our society was a variety, having none with the inhabitants. We fared sumptuously amongst them whilst we remained.

We next went to Tunis with another dispatch, which is a republic and a kingdom of Africa. The manners and customs are much similar to those at Tripoli, in some degree worse. Sodomy is carried on to the greatest height, even in the streets at night. The Bey countenances it more than the Bey of Tripoli and sets an infamous example. His seraglio does not even

consist of an amazing number of wives and concubines but likewise of little boys from the ages of eight
to seventeen upon whom he commits that abominable crime. I could not credit this information until
I had ocular proof of it. I saw in one apartment a
number of these boys and the keeper stuffing them
with flour and water the same as poulterers do
turkeys.

This place abounds with a prodigious number of
wild and ferocious animals. I saw here a rhinoceros,
next to the elephant the most powerful quadruped,
its length twelve feet and a half, height seven, and its
circumference equal to its length. The horn is about
four feet in length, solid and is a formidable instru-
ment for annoyance and defence. It will immediately
rip open the body of its antagonist.

I had an opportunity to see the place where the
famous ancient Carthage stood. A small proportion
of the ruins remain to this day. They have a great
number of Christian slaves who are badly treated,
miserably fed, hard labour and what is still worse
and distressing, the idea of never being liberated.
They make no exception of man, woman or child.

These pirates landed one night in a small island
near Sardinia where I had been on shore, set fire to a
village, plundered and took away every soul from it.
I was near being included in the number, only for
shouting aloud that I was John Engleso, a name that

mostly all foreigners give to Britons; as a token of respect, when the Turks meet us they will salute us with '*Bono John, Bono John*'. They respect us from fear, as we are masters of the sea.

Two slaves escaped on board our ship who we landed safe at Malta. It is a law of England whenever a slave, no consequence whether Turk or Christian, comes under our flag, to set that man free in defiance to any menaces. One of them had a narrow escape for his life. He cohabited with a Mahometan woman, which is punished with death to both parties. She was burnt gradually and he would have been flayed and put under the most excruciating tortures.

We made a short stay and then steered to off Toulon, where we received further orders from Lord Nelson to cruise in the Gulf of Gibraltar, that is between Spain and Barbary, to protect our merchant ships from the enemy's privateers.

We put into Tetuan and Tangiers occasionally to wood, water and provision, where they were not much better than those at Tripoli: that is, a set of barbarian monsters. Two captains of the army, a midshipman and myself, departed from Tetuan (in Africa) in a boat in defiance to thirty of their soldiers. The two former went over on a party of shooting from Gibraltar. On putting their baggage and parcels in our boat, the Moors attempted to detain us until they would acquaint the governor, who was then six miles distant, likewise twilight would have put us to a great inconvenience and trouble to have stopped all night. Before our departure these insolent haughty Moors threatened us in their own language to *bastinado* us, that is beat the soles of our feet with a stick until they would become a complete mash and never capable to carry us afterwards.

We cruised nearly three months without anything material happening, unless we made some desperate attempts to capture the privateers, but all in vain.

At this time we had not commenced hostilities with Spain. Our captain, in a very private manner, transgressed the laws of nations by sending in a boat to set fire to an English ship that had been taken by a privateer, in which he succeeded. Having fagots and every appropriate combustible to set her afire, they repaired on board in a very dark night where she lay close to the Spanish shore. They met with very little resistance as only three Frenchmen were on board, who were instantly shot. Shortly afterwards she was in a blaze and then blew up with a tremendous crash. The Spaniards on shore were in confusion, being unaware of this event. Some of them, as I learned afterwards, supposed it to be the Devil let loose from hell; others thought it was hell itself; the third party was of opinion that it was imps belching flames of fire. We stood off to the Barbary coast, which kept the plan completely concealed.

9. Shipwrecked, March 1804

We anchored in the Bay of Tangiers and in the course of four days set sail in the night and worked up against the wind, to Gibraltar, which was blowing extremely hard.

All that day and part of the night, I was unusually melancholy. After supper we were all enjoying a glass of punch and about ten o'clock our first lieutenant came off deck and said, 'Doctor, you are in extreme danger tonight and I would advise you to take care of yourself.' I laughed at the idea and considered it a jest. I retired to sleep but, lo! at eleven o'clock I was aroused with the dreary shouts of 'all hands ahoy (every person to go upon deck) the ship will be wrecked'.

I just took time to put on a pair of pantaloons and my coat across my arm. When I arrived there, I have not words to express the dismal scene. The night was so dark I could not see ten yards before me. It rained so hard I was wet in one minute. I had hardly time to recover from my sleep and fright when my ears were saluted with the tremendous surging of the sea, which was mountains high against a reef of rocks ahead and on each side of our ship. Reiterated peals of thunder and flashes of lightning brought into view an immense mountain which apparently seemed right above us. The whole firmament was in a state of confusion.

We put our ship about, but all in vain; let go an anchor, that would not bring us up; then we fired signal guns of distress, should any ship be near might assist us – had there been any, none would have even attempted to come within a mile of us. The echo of our signal guns from the mountains, thunder, its echo, great waves dashing against the rocks, its echo, the vivid flashes of lightning which rendered our destruction more conspicuous, alone the human specie, was sufficient to timidate all the Pandemonium or the whole infernal assembly of Devils.

We were driving gradually towards the rocks and, as I only expected a few moments to live, I offered a prayer up to the great Father of Mercies. All trepidation seemed to forsake me and I was for the first time in my life quite reconciled to death. At half past eleven o'clock I may well say with Falconer:

> Horror fraught the dreadful scene draws near
> The ship hangs hovering on the verge of death,
> Hell yawns, rocks rise, and breakers roar beneath
> With mournful looks the seamen eyed the strand,

Where death's inexorable jaws expand.
Uplifted on the surge to heaven she flies,
Her shattered top half buried in the skies
She headlong plunging thunders on the ground.
Earth groans! Air trembles! and the deeps resound.
Her giant bulk the dread concussion feels
And quivering with the wound in torment reels.
So reeled, convulsed with agonizing throes,
The bleeding hull breaks the murdering blows,
Again she plunges! hark! A second shock,
Tears her strong bottom on the marble rock!
Down on the Vale of death with dismal cries,
Fated victims shuddering roll their eyes,
Ha! total night and horror here preside.
My stunn'd ear tingles to the whizzing tide;
It is the funeral knell! And gliding near,
Methinks the phantoms of the dead appear;
But lo! emerging from the watery grave
Again they float incumbent on the wave.
Again the dismal prospects open round,
The wrecks, the shores, the dying and the drowned.
And see! enfeebled by repeated shocks,
Those two scramble on the adjacent rocks
The faithless hold no longer can retain,
They sink overwhelmed and never rise again.[84]

This poem gives a very expressive account, yet to come more into the minutiae, I will continue my narrative. At half past eleven o'clock the 29th February 1804, when reconciled to death and offering my prayers to the Almighty who has saved me in all my perilous situations, both by land and sea and in several battles against the enemies of my country, to take me into his protection at this critical moment, and, as there did not seem any possibility of escaping without his assistance, and if he pleased that my time of dissolution had arrived, to accept me into his Heavenly Kingdom.

She struck one rock with a tremendous crash which throwed us all off our feet. On my recovery from this dreadful shock, a large wave went right over us that rendered me incapable for a time to gain my sight and expel the water I had swallowed, when I clearly perceived the sea had carried us over one ridge of rocks, but alas! we were driving down to a greater reef. Four of our men jumped overboard to swim on shore, but there did not seem the least possibility of them obtaining that length. The best of swimmers could not have any command, as the waves would dash them to pieces against the rocks. One of them I supposed had shared that fate – I heard him groan aloud but suddenly ceased – therefore I conjectured he had suffered for his rash attempt.

Our ship came with another tremendous crash against a rock. I thought every plank she consisted of was stove to atoms. I did not suffer so much from this as I was better prepared by catching the rigging. She again struck as hard when a rock went right through her. All our masts and yards fell instantly. Upon this, we struck hard and fast.

On her heaving to one side, it proved to be a breakwater, together with the ridge of rocks we had wonderfully been carried over. This, since the fatal blow, put on a more prosperous aspect, and gave us hopes of being saved, which cheered our drooping spirits. We had not only the sea to contend with; we ran the hazard of being bruised to pieces by the masts and yards falling. Several of our men were materially hurt from this cause.

All this time I retained my coat across my arm from having the presence of mind that it would cover my nakedness should I be so fortunate as to arrive on shore and I could not reflect that I lost it from neglect. Some of the officers went into their cabins in order to obtain part of their clothes. I ventured into mine to procure £15 in Spanish coin, which would be a useful article to me in Spain. On my return upon deck with a small box that contained it, the ship gave another thump. At that instant the water rushed up to my knees. I dropped it and never appeared there any more. Life is sweet when in danger. Little do we care about the riches of the world. Although I lost £300 worth of things, in clothes, money, surgical instruments, plate, etc. etc., I never once reflected but thanked the Supreme Being for my preservation.

We had only one small jolly boat on board (the other three were left at Gibraltar to be repaired), which was got out with great difficulty. Seven men were ordered to use their utmost endeavours to get on shore and pass a rope round a rock so as to haul the boat off and on to the ship and land the remainder of the crew in safety, in which they succeeded. I went in the second and landed partly in the boat and partly by swimming.

Never upon any occasion were my spirits more exhilarated: the most happy moment I ever enjoyed in my life. Although completely wet for four hours, hardly any clothing, my limbs mangled in several places by the sharp points of the rocks, I never once felt cold or pain. Our captain on the first alarm secured a tinderbox, which was of the utmost utility. As soon as part of the wreck and sails were washed on the beach, we erected a large tent and then kindled a fire, which assisted us in drying the small remnant of our clothes. Two of the men that jumped overboard were missing; the other two arrived on shore with the greatest difficulty, almost senseless from bruises, wounds and loss of blood.

At length the long wished for object arrived, day-light, when we discovered that we were shipwrecked near Cabritta Point on the coast of Spain. On our surveying the dangers we had surmounted, it appeared a miracle to us how we escaped. We found one of the men washed upon the beach with his skull fractured and all his limbs broken. The other we never heard of.

The wind and rain ceased for three hours and then began with its usual fury. She went to pieces about six hours after we left her and every plank separately was driven on shore. The power and providence of God were wonderfully displayed in the preservation of our lives, thus exposed to destruction. He made the sea and the dangers therein, yet at his pleasure saved us in a situation that seemed impossible to mortal man.

We remained there for seven days, wet all the time as it rained incessantly. Four of them we were nearly starved, having nothing to eat but a little barley and a few shellfish. Boats made an attempt to come from Gibraltar. The outrageous and roaring sea prevented them from landing, as the boat would be staved in an instant and consequently every soul perish. We could procure no assistance from Algeciras in Spain on account of rivers that intercepted us, which rose to a prodigious height from the great fall of rain. At last from a short suspension of wind, we were supplied with bread, beef and wine, which just came in time to prevent us from slaying two jackasses we caught in the mountains.

For several days and nights after the shipwreck, I

supposed, and all the reasonable remonstrations with myself could not persuade me to the contrary, but what the rock or rather a small mountain rolled a little. When I communicated my sentiments to the captain and other officers, they were of the same opinion. Yet I still persisted in the impossibility, when the captain replied that the movement of the mountain was not improbable, for he had once been upon a narrow neck of land which had great motion during a storm. The sea, he conjectured, had undermined it, which was the cause of motion and might be the case now.

A man-of-war brig was sent from Gibraltar on the cessation of the storm to take us over, where the officers of the army were very attentive to us, being sensible of our hardships. All my friends congratulated me on my escape. I shall consider myself under everlasting obligations for the polite behaviour of Captains Frederick, Jones, Surgeon McDwyer, Assistant Marmion, Quartermaster Finney, who were all my countryman and belonging to the 54th Irish Regiment of Foot.

I remained here for nearly two months and, although having plenty of amusement and acquaintances, my mind was agitated under the anxiety of procuring a passage in order that I might have the pleasure of seeing my relations in Ireland, being my intention to go there before I should enter into any service again. This, together with every kind of provisions so extremely dear (it cost me half a guinea for my dinner daily) brought me into a determination of travelling through Spain to Portugal, as I could get an immediate passage in a packet[85] if not in a man of war. Before I left Gibraltar I had settled my passage in a merchant ship bound to Cork in Ireland, but the day after I read in a newspaper of a ship being taken off Cork by a French privateer, which timidated and excited me to give up the idea.

I hired a horse and a guide at Algeciras and we rode over a very rugged mountainous country, seldom had a bed to repose on. I should have been glad to have travelled all night and slept during the day on account of the intense heat of the sun, only my guide, who was well acquainted with the road, informed me we should run the risk of either being robbed or murdered. We continued our irksome journey and, when convenient, changed horses. We obtained the length of sixty miles, where we entered a pettifogging inn (to our great discomfort, few of these we met on the road) about twilight and refreshed ourselves. As there was a better inn about ten miles further on our road, I immediately proposed to proceed thither. We had not got on above six miles when we were followed by three men on horseback.

My Spanish guide remembered that these might be

the very three men we had left at the last inn. He did not like their appearance and although he did not communicate it to me, he would not have left at that place tonight, only he took them for robbers. If my suspicions are true, all our money will be taken from us and probably stripped of our clothes. I made him understand, rather than be pillaged in that manner, I would fight them and should lose my life first. I had two pistols, would get my horse against a wall and shoot the first man that came near me. He begged for the love of God and Maria Virginia to desist from that resolution, otherwise in a short time we would be two dead man.

Being a fine moonlight night, we descryed them about half a mile from us. This place was a complete wilderness, not even a house to be seen betwixt the two inns. I must confess my mind was not altogether tranquil but I trusted to the Supreme Being who, after delivering me from so many dangers, would not allow me to be slain by three Spanish banditti. I fired my pistols to show them we were not unprepared, and put a double charge in, and galloped as hard as possible. They followed us for two miles and then returned. Whether we escaped from our horses proving to act like Pegasus[86] or the report of the pistols timidated them is best known to themselves. However, it is well known that any person well armed, having courage, need never be robbed by any thief, for robbers are great cowards when they see their object prepared.

Upon our arrival at the inn, my guide, who was all the time in a terrible fright, wet with perspiration as if dipped in a well of water, gained his courage like all cowards when it was not wanted, swore dreadful oaths: if he had his will, he would flay all the robbers in Spain, torture, gibbet and let them die by piece meals. After venting his tremendous execrations a full quarter of an hour which made the whole house ring, the people stared not only at his words but his frightsome figure, gesticulations, grimaces and distortions of his body – his hair that stood up on an end had not since the fright returned to its normal position – at last he terminated, by all the holy Evangelists, he would not come as guide again for twenty times the sum I gave him.

We sat down to a comfortable supper, for the first time since our departure from Gibraltar, with the landlady and daughter. The latter attracted my attention and I was in temporary love with her from her fine black eyes. In fact she was what I call a charming girl which induced me to stop two nights when I was obliged to bid eternal farewell to *chara angelica mea*, Miss Maria Joulia Tabo. After all my anxiety, I halted here and the only excuse I can form is being a young man of a very sanguine constitution and a strong attachment to the fair sex (although not always in an honourable way) whose allurements have often undermined all my other resolutions, with the exception of my professional studies with which I never once allowed them to interfere.

We jogged on to the frontiers of Portugal and continued our rout to Lisbon, the capital, after eight days absence from Gibraltar. Nothing more in this long journey particularly occurred. My face was so much tanned with the sun I could not with any degree of propriety appear amongst my old acquaintances for a day or two. I heard of a packet about to sail for England, where I went to take my passage but, being asked eighteen guineas for the same, and as she would land me at Falmouth, 265 miles from London, I thought it more prudent to stop a few days and go home in a man of war, which would land me in the Downs only 70 miles from London. This at least saved me £30. I passed a very agreeable month at Lisbon and yet I was at times unsettled and anxious for the day of my departure, which at length, to my profound satisfaction, arrived. I went with Lord M. Carr[87] in the *Fisguard*, man of war.

10. Homecoming, June 1804

WE HAD A TEDIOUS passage and, as I thought, the longest in my life. I landed in June 1804 at Deal, England, after being in a foreign station about six years. My joy in embracing England (I may well say so: on putting my feet on the ground I fell with my hands amongst the pebbles) may be better conceived than expressed.

I entered into a soliloquy, thanking the Father of Mercies for my safe arrival, and congratulating myself on having the opportunity and the pleasure of seeing a great part of the three quarters of the Globe, Europe, Africa and Asia, beside a great number of islands – Minorca, Majorca, St. Peters, Malta, Lampadosa, Sicily, Corsica, Elba, Candia, Cyprus, Rhodes – and several other places, both on the Continent and lesser islands, but as nothing particular occurred to me, I did not conceive it worthy of inserting. I likewise had the honour to be in several desperate battles, both by sea and land, against the enemies of my country, the misfortune to be taken prisoner into France and was very near being blown up by powder, likewise shipwrecked and the fortune to have escaped multitudes of dangers which of course was incident to my way of life, in travelling the sea several hundred thousands of miles which would puzzle a better mathematician than me to calculate; and the two last, although best, a series of good health in all the various climes, and the luck to increase my fortune.

After my long absence, the houses appeared strange and of a new model, much cleaner and neater than those abroad; numerous sets of ladies that parade the streets of Deal, which place is considered to produce as handsome as in any part in England and comparatively superior in appearance, style and manners to all those I had been in the habit of seeing lately; I was enamoured with every prospect alternately.

In the evening I set off post haste to London and arrived the next day. My first object was to get a suit of clothes made in the fashion. What I had were very good but, made in the first fashion abroad, would not answer me in London. In general, strangers are respected from their appearance and any person with an old fashioned coat or waistcoat would be taken for a common mechanic or tradesman. For instance, I went to look for lodgings in Pantons Square near the Haymarket. Upon asking the woman her price, she viewed me from top to toe and, after two or three minutes silence, informed me that I could not have them without a recommendation. I acquainted her who and what I was, that it was not convenient for me to procure one tonight but would perfectly satisfy her in the morning by calling upon my agent. In reply, very scurrilous and with an insolent air: I might come provided I would allow my trunk to be put in her possession until the recommendation would come, for she had a great quantity of plate and several other things of value in her house. It would be very easy for a lodger to rob her. A number of robberies are committed in town the same way, continues she.

I could bear this most impudent, insolent ill-bred wench no longer, and if it were her husband I would ring the nose off his face, and that evil thinkers was evil doers. I did not doubt but what the house contained a gang of thieves. I was confident in this assertion from being an excellent physiognomist and furthermore (staring her in the face) that she had the outlines of a female swindler drawn on her countenance, a procurer and conniver. Then turning round to two of her daughters who had appeared on hearing this instructing dialogue, and of course put in a few words to chime with their mother, addressing the younger: you are a complete jilt from your manner of goggling and squinting; to the elder: you have slept with as many different men as I have fingers to steal your mother's plate and, if I am not very much mistaken, I saw you the other night in the lobby amongst the women of your own class and that you went to a private house with a gentleman of my acquaintance.

N.B. – Lobby, a place in Covent Garden Theatre where all the prostitutes resort during the play. Private house is where the whores and the whoremonger may sleep all night.

They could stand this no longer. One flies to the poker, another to a chair and the third was almost motionless from excessive rage; and I to the door, otherwise I would have received some blows from these amazons. I was in a fit of laughter that I had succeeded so well in retaliating, which made them (woman like) more desperate and, upon the whole, I was glad to get clear of the house without a few clumsy thumps.

I went directly to the opposite door and took lodgings at one guinea and a half per week, where I only remained four days but requested the woman to keep them for me until my return from Ireland, as I would pay her the same as if I stopped. I expressed an inward wish to have a little more fun with these modern amazons.

A taylor promised a to have my clothes made in two days, but the rascal, to my great mortification, kept me waiting five. I set out equipped in the London mode, settled my accounts with my agent, passed my examinations at Surgeon's Hall and procured my Diploma and became a Member of the Royal College of Surgeons, London, 15th day of June 1804.

After considering deliberately, I resolved to enter into the army, wishing to adhere to the resolution I had formed when shipwrecked on the coast of Spain. With this intention, I repaired to the Army Medical Board, but from the absence of the members, I could get no business transacted for a fortnight. I thought it expedient to proceed on my journey to Ireland.

I took my place in the coach for Holyhead in Wales and left the great metropolis a Sunday evening. I was the only passenger in the coach and of course solitary until about half way, when I met with a banker, wife and daughter, who likewise took a passage together with two gentlemen. The lady went with her husband merely to see England the time he was employed to get these new Irish crowns coined, one of which I had the pleasure of seeing before they arrived in Ireland. He went to Liverpool to have them conveyed in a man of war.

I paid great attention to both for three reasons: 1st, it behoves every gentleman to be attentive and extremely polite to the ladies. The female sex claim and have an undoubted right to it. Should we act on the contrary, they will construe it (very reasonably) into want of manners and good breeding, treat you with inward contempt and impute to your ignorance;

2^{ly}, I admired the daughter; 3^{ly}, it would be useful and pleasant to form an acquaintance in Dublin.

Our passengers now consisted of these two ladies, two gentlemen and myself, one of whom seemed to have charge of the ladies. It immediately occurred to me that he was my rival. Now the great question! How was I to ascertain this? I began to meditate on the most rational and polite way of discovery. Nothing can be more vulgar, indeed impertinent, to ask a stranger who or what he is, was my first thought. Upon an accurate investigation, I conjectured that the most probable way would be to introduce different topics and by that means sound them what profession they were, the first favourable opportunity which would tend to make more important discoveries.

I addressed them in the following words: 'Gentlemen, it is a long time since I had the felicity to see Ireland, which is my native country. I should esteem it a particular favour and would oblige me very much to be informed whether the natives, since their late rebellion and union, were in a more or less flourishing state and whether the stable [*sic*] commodity of that place, which I believed was chiefly linen, turned out well to the pecuniary advantage of the people.' When I mentioned linen I touched one of my fellow travellers upon the right string, who replied with an interested air, 'I can give you, sir, any information on the subject.' He commenced, and terminated, by saying he had been at a great fair and sold several hundred pieces of Irish linen.

This discovery perfectly satisfied me that he was a linen jobber. I discussed with him upon 8, 12, 14 and 15 hundreds[88] and my opinion which was the most profitable. That excited him to ask if ever I had been concerned in this branch. I answered with a look of disapprobation in the negative and that my information originated from the extreme pleasure I was endowed with upon scrutinising into the trade of my native country.

I touched my supposed rival upon arts, manufactories, architecture, physic, etc. etc. who answered me extremely polite, seemed different from the other to be a complete gentlemen and man of the world. I began to be dubious whether I should discover his occupation.

The old lady, who was ready to burst all this time to put her tongue in edgeways, at last succeeded in asking how long I had been from Ireland, whether my relations were living and at the same time dropping a sympathising tear: 'I have a son myself that I have not seen this five years, God protect him, wherever he is, if alive; he is a captain in the army.'

In order to get into her good graces, this was too favourable an opportunity to let pass. I discoursed upon morality, the uncertainty of this transitory world, the duty of children to their parents and the necessity of parting for a time, the felicity of meeting again, concluding with a few similitudes[89] and funny anecdotes, which caused the old lady to leave off the melancholy aspect for a smiling countenance and her and I to be particular friends during the remainder of the journey.

All this loquacity did not prevent me from the chief object, that is, attention to the young lady I was desirous to follow. *Suaviter in modo fortiter in re.*[90]

At length we arrived in Wales, which is so much admired for the simplicity and honesty of the people and mountainous and grotesque appearance of the country, where we all sat down to a comfortable dinner and agreed very well, except the linen jobber, who was extremely fractious and ill tempered, even the whole way, to the great discomposure of the ladies. Although a complete goddess before him, no, not all the soft expressions of Venus and Daphne would mollify his temper, which I conjectured originated from being obliged to be at so great an expense while in our company. He disliked the pastry, tarts and various kinds of fruits after a good substantial dinner, which he considered unnecessary dishes and, of course, unnecessary expenses, but when I called for a bottle of sherry wine and one of port, he could not contain his sentiments any longer.

I begged that he would not give himself any further

trouble or uneasiness as I should pay for the wine; it was not my wish to put any person to an expense they could not afford, at the same time throwing a side glance to the remainder of our company who enjoyed it greatly to see him so much chagrined. After this satiric, he got into a terrible rage and swore he could afford a bottle of wine as well as any man in England. 'I do not know who the devil you are, but I think better than you,' looking at me and walking out of the room. We all laughed heartily and unanimously agreed to have more expensive dinners for the future.

To excite more diversion, I gave the waiter a shilling extraordinary to ask the jobber, in our presence, for the usual acknowledgement that he was in the habit of receiving from all travellers, and not to take less than a shilling. The old lady was so well pleased with this scheme that she gave him another to put it in full force. The waiter was as good as his word, asked him with his hand extended to his hat, for a small compliment in recompense for attending him at dinner.

Says he, 'D–m you altogether; there is a sixpence and do not give me any more trouble.' The waiter in reply informed him laconically, if he could not afford him any more than that small sum, to keep it, as it would be of service to him on the road. The jobber flung the sixpence at his head and vented terrible execrations and vengeance against them all for a set of impostors and extortioners. We endeavoured to stifle our laughing but could not contain ourselves any longer, were obliged to laugh aloud until our sides ached. He became sulky and never opened his lips for the remainder of the day.

We had now arrived at Carnarvonshire, which is so remarkable for Snowdon Mountain, moors, chasms and lakes, that make it a very dreary region. I began to be extremely fatigued: no wonder, as I had not closed my eyes for three nights. I was a little consoled being informed that the coach would stop all night at Bangor. I had come at the rate of seven miles an hour ever since my departure from London. Indeed, at all events, it was my intention to have remained a night at Bangor and take a post chaise from there at my own expense, rather than go without another night's sleep.

By this time I had discovered the gentleman's profession. After discussing upon several topics, I at last brought in the navy and army, our different colonies abroad, which at last touched him upon the right string. He had been captain in the army, was in the Mediterranean, knew some of my acquaintance, went from thence to the West Indies. A fortune being left him, he returned to Dublin, married a lady, so I considered him no more my competitor. He gave me a strong invitation to spend a week with him, which I promised on my return from Dublin.

Upon our arrival at Bangor, we excluded the jobber from our tea party. After indulging ourselves with this infusion, I proposed to take a walk to an antique castle, as we should have time before dark, remarking that the married and single ought to walk together, which gave me an opportunity to make some soft expressions and enter *gradatim* into the esteem of the young one. We were highly delighted with this prospect, together with the Welsh women wearing the same kind of hats as the men.

The next morning we passed over the narrow strait of water in a boat called Menai to the island of Anglesey (famous for once being the place of the Druids) where there was a coach ready for us, and that evening arrived in Holyhead, where we had a most cheerful dinner and my spirits highly exhilarated on the idea of being in old Ireland the next day. I began already to smell the turf.

The sailing of the packet boat was announced and all the passengers anxiously employed themselves to send sufficient provisions on board for their passage. Seeing such an amazing quantity of hams, fowls, tongues, mutton, beef, veal, wine, rum, brandy and porter go on board for gentlemen and ladies that had not been accustomed to the sea, I did not conceive it requisite to send any of these articles as it would be only lumber, and, besides, the boiled hams and fowls would find me to be the only customer, which proved to be actually the case. They were all sick and I fared sumptuously. I took care that my two female companions wanted for no delicacy that would agree with their stomachs.

The wind being contrary, it was the following evening before I had the pleasure of beholding my native land. The first was the mountains of Wicklow and the gentle rising hills of Clantorf, which excited gentle rising emotions in my breast. At twilight we anchored in Dublin harbour near the Pigeon House.[91]

All the passengers were extremely anxious as to who would get onshore first to secure a place in the long coach that was waiting for us (first come, first served on these occasions). My two female friends were particularly interested: if they could not succeed, they would be obliged to stop to a late hour of the night until their own carriage would come. I begged them to remain perfectly easy on this point as I would take care to procure a seat for them by this present vehicle.

All the gentlemen were in a state of confusion, jumping into the boat until at last she was full. On our arrival to the shore, I slipped a shilling into one of the sailor's hand that pulled the boat, at the same time making use of some sea expressions. They favoured my design but, as I was in my element, the time they were thinking about it, I jumped out of the boat and when I got one foot upon the steps, I employed the other to shove the boat off, pretending that I had stumbled. It required at least three minutes before they could bring her to the same position. In consequence of this scheme, a nobleman fell with his feet into the water and would have been completely ducked only for a sailor that catched him.

I secured three seats in the long coach and afterwards had plenty of time to laugh at their great bustle in landing.

About half past nine we got to Dublin where I called for a hackney coach and accompanied my two female friends to their own elegant house and had supper with them, and for the first time informed them who I was, when they made me a promise to spend a week or a fortnight on my return to Dublin. From thence I went to an inn to procure a passage in the stage coach to Dundalk, but afterwards had great difficulty to get a bed in that part of the town. I went to five or six different inns but could not succeed as all the beds were engaged, in one of which I met the jobber, who had the laugh against me as he was an old traveller on this road and the first thing he did was to make *bonnum securum* of a bed.

An account of this city which I have often heard occurred to me: that is, the want of good inns and accommodations for travellers is a subject (and no wonder) of universal complaint. I repaired to the inn where the coach set out from in the morning to sleep on two chairs rather than miss my passage.

Money, which is the panacea or absolute remedy among the lower class of people for worldly things, proved now to be my friend. I slipped 5s. into the servant maid's hand to let me have her bed and at the same time giving her a hint to put clean sheets on. I dare presume to assert that for twice as much more, this buxom chambermaid would have been my bed-fellow all night. This is often practised in the inns of England, but of course kept secret from the masters.

At length the dawn appeared, to my great joy, when I set off for Dundalk and left this great metropolis I may say without even seeing it. As the coach turned off to the Armagh road at Dundalk, I was obliged to take a post chaise from this. An elderly lady joined me who had come from England to obtain a little property left her. She had come from Newry that morning to get a passage at Dundalk for England in place of going to Warren's Point. I could not help smiling at her mistake. Indeed she could not avoid it herself, remarking jocosely that since she had been in Ireland, she had been partly initiated to their manner: that is, blundering. To make blunders is undoubtedly the characteristic of the Irish and, from my knowledge, they are more guilty of it (in their expressions) than any other nation. Many a funny anecdote is related and printed about this.

The nearer I approached to Donaghmore, the more my anxiety increased to see my relations; at times in the greatest suspense as to whether they were alive, and others timidated to ask lest some of their deaths would be announced. At last I gained all my fortitude and enquired at the top of Bars Hill of a complete mountaineer and, although he lived very near, he did not know a family of the Lowrys in the whole country, which excited me to suppose that they were all extinct, but shortly after this the pleasure of seeing them may be better conceived than expressed.

Notes

1 According to Mr. H. Laughlin, Verger of All Saints Church, Maidstone, Kent, registers of that Church record the burial of James Lowry, Earl Street, 13 February 1855.

2 According to Mr. Joseph P. Robinson, Superintendent Registrar at Omagh, County Tyrone, Ireland, this is Clananees Glebe, near Castlecaulfield; a glebe being a portion of land going with clergyman's benefice, which accounts for its not being shown on any geographical map of Ireland.

3 According to the Kent County Archivist, Mr. Felix Hull, the Land Transfer Records show Dr. James Lowry as the occupier of a house in Earl Street (then Bullock Street) Maidstone, Kent, from 1816 onwards.

4 The year in which Napoleon, following his victories in Italy, was appointed by the Directory to be Commander-in-Chief of the Army of England, then preparing along the French Channel coast for the invasion of the British Isles.

5 In the London dockland.

6 A division of the Navy Board (the Royal Navy's administrative bureaucracy) specifically concerned with the health of seamen. They ran the naval hospitals and were responsible for appointing surgeons to the fleet.

7 An 80-gun ship built at Plymouth in 1798 and one of the largest two-decker ships of the line in the British fleet. She had been intended to be Lord Nelson's flagship from the start but as she was not ready in time to allow Nelson to join Lord St. Vincent, who was off Cadiz blockading the Spanish fleet, Lord Nelson hoisted his flag on board the *Vanguard* on 10 April 1798. He transferred to the *Foudroyant* at Naples in June 1799.

8 While the seamen slept in the familiar hammocks, officers usually slept in cots similarly suspended from the deckhead. To some the motion of these is not comfortable, and many of the permanent crew of the current *Endeavour* replica, for example, prefer hammocks.

9 Sir Thomas Byard.

10 The French squadron under Commodore J.B.M. Bompart consisted of a 74-gun line of battle ship and nine frigates. They were intending to lend support to an Irish uprising.

11 Sir John Borlase [*sic*] Warren was already a successful commander of detached squadrons, and his force defeated the French in this action off Donegal, 11 October 1798. Later Lowry calls him Borlus Warren; indeed, many of his contemporaries had difficulties with the correct spelling of his middle name.

12 Both 74-gun ships, although the French ship was larger. After capture, the latter was renamed *Donegal* and became something of a favourite ship, being retained in active service until the 1840s.

13 Captured ships were sold and the value divided between officers and men of those ships involved in taking the prize ship or ships. For warships taken or destroyed there was also 'head and gun money', a bounty based on the size of the enemy crew at the start of the action. Prize receipts were on a sliding scale according to rank. For surgeon's mates this was one-eighth of the net total, but shared with the midshipmen, sergeants of Marines, and some of the senior petty officers. Since prize money might well exceed a year's salary, it was regarded much like winning the lottery.

14 About 20 miles south-west of Gibraltar.

15 The guns of the period were denominated by the weight of shot they fired. A 32-pounder was the largest calibre regularly carried in British ships of the line, so it was not an insignificant weapon by which to be fired on.

16 Lowry had not previously mentioned that *Foudroyant* was the flagship of Vice Admiral Lord Keith. For some time Keith deputised for the ailing Commander-in-Chief of the Mediterranean Fleet, Earl St Vincent, and eventually succeeded him in January 1800.

17 Admiral Lord St. Vincent heard on 30 May 1799 that the French fleet had left Toulon and, fearing for Nelson at Naples, he detached Rear Admiral Duckworth with the *Leviathan*, *Foudroyant*, *Northumberland* and *Majestic* to reinforce Nelson at Naples

18 A 74-gun ship launched in 1787. Lowry transferred to the *Swiftsure* on 17 June 1799.

19 This 100-gun First Rate, launched in 1790, was the Royal Navy's greatest loss from any cause during the wars of 1793-1815. However, Lowry exaggerates the casualties, modern research putting the figure around 690.

20 Benjamin Hallowell. This American-born officer was one of

Nelson's 'Band of Brothers', who had fought at the Nile (and before that at St. Vincent and Corsica). His highly distinguished career culminated in a knighthood and the rank of admiral.

21 This unlikely-sounding incident is actually recorded by several eyewitnesses as having occurred in June 1799 (see, for example, Lt. G S Parsons, *Nelsonian Reminiscences*, reprint 1998, pp3-4). The corpse was that of Francisco Caracciolo, a prince of ancient Greek descent, who had been Commodore of the Neapolitan Navy. He was tried and found guilty of treason at a court martial held (some say improperly) on the *Foudroyant*. In what is still the most controversial episode in his career, Nelson is alleged to have signed the order that he be hanged from the yardarm of the Sicilian frigate *Minerva* in the Bay of Naples.

22 Latin had been the *lingua franca* of educated Europe and it is interesting that as late as the first years of the nineteenth century it was useful to Lowry in any country where he could find a priest of the Roman Catholic Church.

23 Famously to become the mistress of Nelson and mother of his daughter Horatia, although Lowry says nothing that suggests he knew of the liaison.

24 One of the fortified ports from which French troops embarked for Egypt; 35 miles north-west of Rome.

25 Captain John Nicholson Inglefield [*sic*].

26 Sir Richard Bickerton Bart. had seen action in the American Revolutionary War, becoming a post captain in 1781. He was promoted to rear admiral in 1799 and rose to be a full admiral and commissioner of the Admiralty later in the Napoleonic War.

27 The United States was at that time actively engaged in naval conflict, but because it was never formally declared it is known to history as the Quasi-War with France. It was essentially a trade war, the would-be neutral America trying to defend its carrying trade against the depredations of French commerce raiders.

28 The biblical story of the ass divinely inspired to speak is in Numbers 22.

29 The Roman god of sleep.

30 This anachronistic term, left over from the sixteenth century, was reserved for any Spanish ship suspected of carrying 'treasure' from the New World.

31 The popular version of this event was that when the Spanish Governor Morla appealed to the English commander to spare the town 'the gallant Englishman, ever generous to a suppliant foe, sailed away'. The explanation given by Keith's Captain of the Fleet, Philip Beaver, however, read as follows: 'Independent of the

objection which a dreadful malady, called by some the plague and by others the yellow fever, opposed to our disembarking, the late season of the year, the danger of the coast, and the difficulty of communication between the soldiers and sailors were deemed sufficient by the two commanders-in-chief to relinquish the attempt.' Whether or not Lowry's version of this episode of 4 October 1800 was closer to the truth, it is a matter of historic record that it was severely criticised by the Government on the ground that Abercromby's army could have been better employed in the Mediterranean. As Lowry says at the end of the preceding paragraph, this expedition eventually landed in Egypt and forced the surrender of the French troops occupying the country.

32 Marmaris, now a popular holiday destination on the south-western coast of Turkey. The fleet of seven sail of the line, frigates and sixty to seventy transports arrived here on 31 January 1801. As Lowry says, Abercromby used the time here to train and exercise his army in the techniques of amphibious warfare.

33 Ancient measurement 18 to 22 inches (length of forearm).

34 Despite the twisted syntax, from the context Lowry appears to be saying that Asia exceeds Europe and Africa in fertility.

35 Now spelt Cerastes, an eastern horned viper which hides in the sand.

36 Psalm 58: 'Which will not hearken to the voice of charmers'.
    Ecclesiastes 10:11: 'Surely the serpent will bite without enchantment'.
    Jeremiah 8:17: 'For, behold I will send serpents, cockatrices, among you which will not be charmed and they shall bite you, said the Lord.'

37 Joshua 10:11.

38 Alexandria was an ancient city, the seaport of Egypt, about 14 miles west of the Canopic mouth of the Nile; founded by and named after Alexander the Great in 332 BC. It was captured by Napoleonic forces on 2 July 1798. Nelson's victory, usually called the Nile, took place in Aboukir Bay, about 13 miles north-east of Alexandria on 1 August 1798, when most of the French battle-fleet was captured or destroyed, effectively marooning Napoleon's forces in Egypt.

39 Abercromby had 16,000 men in this convoy. The French, under General Menou, had about twice this number, but spread throughout Egypt.

40 The French for calabash – a kind of gourd for holding liquids.

41 Battle of Mandara. The French forces, inferior in number, were commanded by Lanusse.

42 Dysentery.

43 General Menou led a surprise attack with the main French force near Alexandria. Leading from the front, Abercromby [the correct spelling of his name] was killed, but the British gained a hard-fought victory.

44 That part of ancient Egypt which Pharoah presented to Joseph's kindred; appears to have lain between the eastern delta of the Nile and the isthmus of Suez.

45 Genesis 32:28 and 46:29.

46 An ancient Roman fortress on the site of which Cairo was built.

47 Copts. The ancient Christian church of Egypt.

48 On the Nile nine miles from the sea, it is now famous for the discovery there of the Rosetta Stone by French soldiers in 1799. The tablet contains text in three parallel scripts and was the key to deciphering ancient Egyptian hieroglyphs.

49 The Septuagint was a Greek version of the Old Testament including the Apocrypha, said to have been made in 270 BC by seventy-two Hebrew translators. Ptolemy Philadelphus (285-247 BC), the ruler of Egypt, was a renowned patron of learning.

50 Philo of Alexandria was a Jewish philosopher born about 20 BC; Justin Martyr was a Christian apologist, born in Palestine AD100 and executed in Rome AD 165; Dr Humphrey Prideaux was an English scholar and divine (1648-1724).

51 A cutter, 14 guns, 215 tons; ex-French *Mutine* captured 1779. Later Lowry implies the vessel carried 18 guns, 18pdrs (presumably carronades, which were shorter and lighter than conventional cannon).

52 Coast of North Africa.

53 This French squadron was commanded by Admiral Ganteaume. Off the coast of Crete (Candia), it captured the *Swiftsure* on 24 June 1801, which became one of only four British ships of the line to surrender during the wars of 1793-1815. The ship was recaptured at Trafalgar in 1805.

54 Arrival at Toulon was on 22 July 1801.

55 Until Napoleon unilaterally abolished the convention, it was usual for belligerent nations to exchange prisoners of war (especially officers) for equal numbers of men of similar rank. Cartels were ships expressly taken up for the purpose of exchanging prisoners and they were allowed free passage. Minorca, which had been held by the British from 1708 to 1756 and from 1764 to 1781, was again captured in 1798. Its principal attraction was the magnificent harbour of Port Mahon, where they had built extensive naval facilities, including a hospital.

56 Now part of Tel Aviv, located on the coast thirty-seven miles north-west of Jerusalem. It was where the cold-blooded slaughter of over 4000 Turkish prisoners had taken place in 1799 after Napoleon had promised them amnesty if they surrendered. Traditionally, this is also the place where Jonah, when embarking for Spain, was swallowed by a big fish.

57 Janissaries: originally an elite corps of the Ottoman army recruited from Christian slaves and captives, but by this date the term was used loosely for any Turkish soldiers.

58 So termed by ancient Greek writers.

59 An ancient Greek city of Asia Minor and home to the largest temple of the ancient world.

60 A technical term in fortification: a structure intended to be invulnerable to high-trajectory explosive shells (known as at the time as 'bombs').

61 The Peace of Amiens had been signed on 1 October 1801 but it was not ratified until 25 March 1802, and even then it proved but a short-lived truce, Britain declaring war again in May 1803.

62 A 12-gun brig of 213 tons purchased in 1799.

63 Acts 27, 28.

64 It was actually in 1693.

65 Syracuse was founded in 733 BC; Archimedes was born there about 287 BC. Dionysius was 'Tyrant' (autocratic ruler) of Syracuse from about 432 to 367 BC.

66 Pope Pius VII.

67 The Marina was a terrace or promenade about 80 yards wide stretching about a mile along the bay.

68 Captain John Gore was immensely wealthy, being one of the Navy's luckiest officers with regard to prize money.

69 This custom was remarked upon with surprise by many British naval officers visiting Italy. See, for an example from an earlier period, *Augustus Hervey's Journal* (reprinted London 2002), p133.

70 Nymphomania.

71 The sudatorium of a Roman baths was the chamber in which hot air or steam was used to induce sweating; a sudatory was a medicine designed to produce the same effect.

72 This is supposed to have given Captain Lord Cochrane the idea for the employment of poisonous gas as a weapon of war. This was rejected by the Admiralty during the war against Napoleon and again during the Crimean War when as an old man Cochrane revived the proposal.

73 Lawrence Sterne, *A Sentimental Journey through France and Italy* (London 1768).

74 Modern Agrigento.
75 *Incidit in Scyllam, cupiens vitare Charybdim.* Proverbial, based on Virgil, *Aenead* III.
76 *experentia docet*: experience teaches.
77 Mazzaea, a walled cathedral coast town, thirty-two miles from Trapani.
78 Lampedusa.
79 The Ottoman Sultan.
80 On the renewal of war by Britain, Napoleon decreed the internment of all British citizens on French soil. Although this is now common practice, at the time it was regarded as a breach of existing convention that civilians be allowed to return home on the outbreak of war.
81 Roughly speaking, the area of the Libyan desert.
82 The Swedish botanist Carl Linnaeus (1707-1778) whose work laid the foundations of the modern system of taxonomy used in the life sciences.
83 Lowry means Taranto was a city of the Neapolitan state, not part of Naples itself. The tarantella, a folk dance which survives to this day, was believed to cure the bite of the tarantula.
84 Lines from William Falconer (1732-69), *The Shipwreck*, a long poem in three books based on personal experience. Lowry omits couplets and conflates stanzas so may be quoting from memory. It was a very well-known work among seamen, and phrases from it appear frequently in the nautical correspondence of the time.
85 Fast vessels running a regular service, primarily to carry mail but also providing limited passenger accommodation.
86 The mythological winged horse.
87 Actually Lord Mark Kerr, but Lowry's spelling indicates the pronunciation. *Fisguard* was a 38-gun frigate taken from the French in 1797.
88 The quality of linen was distinguished by the number of threads contained in one yard's breadth; thus an eight hundred web is one whose warp contains that number of threads of yarn. Therefore, the higher the number the finer the linen.
89 Impersonations.
90 Gently in manner, resolute in execution.
91 Pigeon House On the end of the South Bull Wall, the usual place to land passengers and mail en route to Dublin city.

Index

Index